PENGUIN  CLASSICS

PROTAGORAS AND MENO

ADVISORY EDITOR: BETTY RADICE

PLATO (c. 429–347 B.C.) stands with Socrates and Aristotle as one of the shapers of the whole intellectual tradition of the West. He came from a family that had long played a prominent part in Athenian politics, and it would have been natural for him to follow the same course. He declined to do so, however, disgusted by the violence and corruption of Athenian political life, and sickened especially by the execution in 399 of his friend and teacher, Socrates. Inspired by Socrates' inquiries into the nature of ethical standards, Plato sought a cure for the ills of society not in politics but in philosophy, and arrived at his fundamental and lasting conviction that those ills would never cease until philosophers became rulers or rulers philosophers. At an uncertain date in the early fourth century B.C. he founded in Athens the Academy, the first permanent institution devoted to philosophical research and teaching, and the prototype of all western universities. He travelled extensively, notably to Sicily as political adviser to Dionysius II, ruler of Syracuse.

Plato wrote over 20 philosophical dialogues like the *Protagoras* and *Meno*, and there are also extant under his name 13 letters, whose genuineness is keenly disputed. His literary activity extended over perhaps half a century; few other writers have exploited so effectively the grace and precision, the flexibility and power, of Greek prose.

W. K. C. GUTHRIE was born in London in 1906 and educated at Dulwich College and Trinity College, Cambridge. He was a Fellow of Peterhouse from 1932 unto 1957, when he became Master of Downing College, a post which he held until 1972. He was also Laurence Professor of Ancient Philosophy in the University of Cambridge. Between 1962 and 1978 he published five volumes of his *History of Greek Philosophy*. Other works include *Orpheus and Greek Religions*, *The Greeks and Their Gods*, *The Greek Philosophers from Thales to Aristotle*, *In the Beginning: some Greek views on the origins of life and the early state of man* (some lectures at Cornell), and he also contributed to various classical journals. Professor Guthrie died in 1981.

PLATO

*

PROTAGORAS
and
MENO

TRANSLATED BY
W. K. C. GUTHRIE

PENGUIN BOOKS

Penguin Books Ltd, Harmondsworth, Middlesex, England
Viking Penguin Inc., 40 West 23rd Street, New York, New York 10010, U.S.A.
Penguin Books Australia Ltd, Ringwood, Victoria, Australia
Penguin Books Canada Ltd, 2801 John Street, Markham, Ontario, Canada L3R 1B4
Penguin Books (N.Z.) Ltd, 182–190 Wairau Road, Auckland 10, New Zealand

—

This translation first published 1956
Reprinted 1961, 1964, 1966, 1968, 1970, 1972, 1974, 1975, 1976,
1977, 1979, 1980, 1981, 1982, 1983, 1985

—

Copyright © W. K. C. Guthrie, 1956
All rights reserved

—

Set, printed and bound in Great Britain by
Cox & Wyman Ltd, Reading
Set in Monotype Garamond

Except in the United States of America,
this book is sold subject to the condition
that it shall not, by way of trade or otherwise,
be lent, re-sold, hired out, or otherwise circulated
without the publisher's prior consent in any form of
binding or cover other than that in which it is
published and without a similar condition
including this condition being imposed
on the subsequent purchaser

CONTENTS

INTRODUCTION

THE *Protagoras* and *Meno* are two of the most enjoyable and readable of Plato's dialogues. Whatever one may think of the philosophical content and the methods of argument employed in the *Protagoras*, it is universally acknowledged to be a dramatic masterpiece. It introduces an unusually large number of characters, and lively, accurate portraiture obviously ranked high among its author's aims. The portraits are drawn with humour and a keen appreciation of personal foibles, but the caricature is not overdone, and one is left with no doubt at all that this is substantially what the living men were like, and that by introducing us not only to their ideas but to their mannerisms, turns of speech and little vanities Plato has done more than would have been possible by any other means to make us personally acquainted with some of the leading figures of thought and life in fifth-century Athens.

Much of the secret of this lies in the stylistic device of the reported dialogue. The dialogue form conveys the dramatic sense of actual presence, whereas the fact that the dialogue is not presented directly, but narrated by Socrates to a friend, allows also for a lively description of scene and actors. It involves, of course, acceptance of the improbability that Socrates could remember by heart the conversation of some hours, including several long and elaborate single speeches. But this is a convention of which one is hardly conscious in reading, and makes no greater demands than do many novels written in the first person. In the *Meno*, where the dramatic element plays a smaller part, this device is not used. We read the whole dialogue like the text of a play. With the *Protagoras* we seem, not simply to read the play, but to see it acted; and when one considers its characters and setting, it is a marvel of good fortune that we should possess this particular first-hand document of life and thought in the great age of Athens. We enter the house of a rich and cultured citizen and find him entertaining the leading Sophists of the time. We see each of these brilliant and egotistic characters behaving in his most characteristic way, and observe among their audience, besides the wealthy patron Callias, such notable figures as Alcibiades, Critias, Charmides, and the two sons of Pericles. We may certainly feel grateful to Plato for giving us the opportunity of sitting in the midst of this remarkable circle and overhearing their conversation.

But in proportion as it excites our admiration as a literary work, so the *Protagoras* perplexes those who would extract its philosophical lesson. This is not because of the depth and difficulty of the problems with which it deals. In that respect we find nothing comparable to the abstruse questions of logic, epistemology, and ontology with which Plato wrestles in later dialogues. But as the philosophy grew deeper and more serious, so the dramatic and literary interest of his works receded into the background. He retained the dialogue form, but it became more and more the vehicle for continuous exposition of one or another philosophical theme. The interest in character-drawing and in the clash of conflicting personalities, which is such a marked and attractive feature of the *Protagoras* and by no means absent from the *Meno*, practically disappears.

When a philosopher expounds his thoughts in the more usual form of a systematic treatise, it may be profound and difficult, but at least the reader's task is limited to finding out what it means on the assumption that the writer was doing his best to communicate his own views in as clear and orderly a manner as possible. But in dealing with something that so far from being a treatise, is a unique amalgam of philosophical discussion with dramatic art, humorous irony, and poetic myth, a number of prior questions must arise. What is Plato trying to do in the *Protagoras*? Is he trying to set forth philosophical ideas of his own? If so, they seem to be surprisingly well disguised. Is he trying to tell us the philosophical views of Socrates, the chief speaker? An endless controversy has been aroused by the fact that in this dialogue he apparently makes Socrates enunciate and defend a doctrine regarded by many as the direct antithesis of what Socrates is likely to have taught in real life. Is he trying to show that, however outrageous a thesis Socrates chose to put forward, he could beat the Sophists at their own style of argument? Or does he aim only at putting on record some of the brilliant talk of that golden age of conversation which was just over, and giving us, mainly through their own mouths, character-sketches of its leading spirits? Is the main purpose of this dialogue dramatic, and not philosophical at all?

In spite of the importance of the dramatic element, it would be difficult to maintain that the work has not a serious philosophical, and in particular an ethical, purpose. Its main subject is the same as that of the *Meno*. Both discuss the question: 'Can virtue be taught?' In other words, what is the secret of that peculiar quality which makes some men so much more proficient than others in the art of living according to the highest human capacities? Why do some make a success of life and others a failure? Is it something we are born with or can it be acquired by taking thought, or instilled by the kind of instruction that a father gives his son or a master his pupil? We cannot doubt that this question, which first came to the fore in the democratic atmosphere of fifth-century Athens, retained its serious import for Plato, as it did for Aristotle after him. But that does not settle the essential questions of how far Socrates is supposed to be speaking seriously, or what is Plato's view about the issues raised; questions inherent in the dramatic form, which in most philosophical literature do not arise. Most of the value of a Platonic dialogue, at least of the early or middle period, lies in the direct impression which it makes on a reader. It cannot be analysed and presented as a collection of neatly tied and labelled parcels of philosophical doctrine. At least, to do so would be to travesty Plato, who made it clear that he did not believe philosophy

could be retailed in that way. It could only be a product of
living contact between mind and mind, in which one strikes
sparks from the other as steel from flint. To write dialogues
was a second best course. Although no substitute for the
direct and dynamic give-and-take between living people,
they provided the only means by which he could reach a
wider circle than that of his personal disciples, to say nothing of posterity down to the twentieth century A.D., and
they at least avoid the defects (in his view) of continuous
treatises which try to expound philosophy 'like any other
subject of instruction'. We cannot in any case participate
in those conversations which he regarded as the ideal
method of philosophical progress, but through the dialogues we learn how they were conducted and watch them
unfold. The dialogues are wholes, and must be treated as
such. To try to strip off, as if they were husks or orna-
mental accretions, the character-drawing or the myth, and
expect to be left with a hard kernel of something which we
can call 'Plato's philosophy', is wasted labour. To some
this may seem a pity, but more than anything else it explains the inexhaustible fascination of the dialogues, their
perennial freshness, and the fact that they are under as lively
discussion today as they were in any previous age.

The *Protagoras* and the *Meno*, as we have noted, differ in
their dramatic technique. The *Meno* plunges straight *in
medias res* with the abrupt question of Meno: 'Tell me,
Socrates, is virtue teachable or not?' This is the question
which the *Protagoras* also raises, but by no means at once.
We have an opening dialogue, or prologue, at Socrates's
house before we even approach the scene of the main conversation. When we get there the setting is described and
the chief persons present are enumerated and character-
ized. Since, as we have seen, the form and content of a
Platonic dialogue are not to be separated, these external
differences (as some would call them) must be borne in
mind in considering the scope and purpose of the two. It
has been argued that the abrupt opening of the *Meno* indi-

cates an early date of composition, before Plato's talent for dramatic representation had reached maturity. On the contrary, Meno's impetuous plunge, with no preliminary courtesies, into a string of questions is dramatically perfect. It gives his character in a nutshell, a character which he sustains throughout the dialogue and on which Socrates gently teases him from time to time. His good looks and charm, he tells him, would be obvious even to a blind man from his employment of the imperious and wayward tone of one accustomed to having his own way. By other touches also Plato shows his mastery of the art of dramatic conversation: the annoyance of Meno at his helplessness in Socrates's hands, expressed in the comparison of his tormentor to an electric fish (a comparison extending to physical features), or the dramatic irony of the exchanges with Anytus and Socrates's closing remark to Meno, when read in the knowledge that Anytus was to be an accuser of Socrates at the forthcoming trial which led to his death. More important, however, than these uncertain considerations of the degree of literary accomplishment displayed, if we are interested in the relative dates of our dialogues, is the fact that the *Meno* shows a distinct advance in philosophical ideas; and to their philosophical content and background we must now turn.

The question of the nature of virtue, and the need which Socrates and Plato felt to decide whether it was a possible subject of instruction, arose from the teaching of the Sophists, those free-lance professors who travelled from city to city in Greece making their living out of the new demand for education. A new social order was calling into being this need of education for citizenship, and particularly for political leadership, which was not provided for by any system of schools or colleges in the cities themselves. This was true especially of democratic Athens, and in Athens the Sophists obviously found the best market and the most congenial intellectual atmosphere. They claimed to provide instruction in a variety of subjects, but particularly in oratory and the kind of intellectual culture needed as a training for public life. Brilliant speakers and instructors as they were, they became the dominant educational influence in the latter half of the fifth century, especially among the more talented and wealthy families, who were naturally best able to afford their fees. Plato often refers to them collectively as 'the teachers of *arete*', *arete* being that word which we translate 'virtue', but which Protagoras, himself a professed teacher of it, is made to describe in the dialogue as 'the proper care of one's personal affairs, so as best to manage one's own household, and also of the State's affairs, so as to become a real power in the city, both as speaker and as man of action'.

The outlook of these men was predominantly secular and sceptical. Law, hitherto believed to have been delivered by Zeus through his son Apollo at the Delphic shrine, was to them no more than 'inventions of good lawgivers of ancient times' (*Protagoras* 326D). To most of them the attempts of previous philosophers to understand 'the nature of things' were a waste of time. Practical life was what mattered, and one could learn how to live without bothering one's head to find out whether the world was the product of divine mind or the fortuitous result of collisions between innumerable atoms blindly jostling one another in infinite space – questions which, in any case, it was probably beyond the wit of man to answer.

This was all very well so far as it went. Socrates too regarded cosmic speculation as an unpractical waste of time. And yet Professor Sinclair was right to describe the difference between Socrates and the greatest of the Sophists, Protagoras, as being 'that Socrates did not regard education and philosophy as a training how to do things, but as a process of acquiring a knowledge of the nature of things'.*

The 'things' in which Socrates was interested were not physical objects but moral qualities. Hitherto, moral terms

* *A History of Greek Political Thought* (Routledge 1951) p. 94; second ed. 1967.

like virtue, justice, courage had been used as freely as they are today, but with no philosophical reflection on the implications of using them. Most people, then as now, if asked a question like 'Is there such a thing as justice?' or 'Do you believe in such a thing as courage?' would answer in the affirmative. Protagoras himself, who denied any universal or absolute validity to moral values, assents to the question of Socrates: 'Is there such a thing as holiness?' even when it is repeated in the form 'Meaning that holiness is an actual thing?' This is a quotation from Plato's dialogue (330D), but it is unlikely to misrepresent Protagoras. To answer 'No' when asked 'Is there such a thing as courage?' would seem absurd to any sensible man.

Well and good, said Socrates, but we must look at the consequences. Here are our orators, and other people, talking about loyalty, freedom, equality, and other fine things as if they meant the same for everybody everywhere, yet men like Protagoras deny that such conceptions have any universal validity. We are each entitled to our private notion of them, which remains true for us so long as we hold it. If that is so, people ought to be stopped from using them as if they were absolutes. The situation is intolerable both intellectually – for it obviously leads to confusion of thought – and morally, since in such a situation there is no means of knowing what constitutes right action. An inquiry is urgently necessary into the nature of moral entities.

Socrates was convinced that the relativist's explanation was wrong, but how was he to prove it? The first step was to get representative people from different walks of life, who all made use of these common general terms, to say simply and clearly what they meant by them. This would at least provide a basis on which some conclusion might be built. And so he set out on the career of interrogation which largely contributed to his unpopularity. Politicians, poets, generals, and craftsmen all came under his scrutiny, and to his dismay, so he said, he discovered that none of them knew the meaning of the words they used, except the craftsmen. These could explain the technical terms incidental to their craft, but spoilt the effect by claiming to know the meaning of wider terms as well, of which his examination proved them to be ignorant.

The political implications of this seemingly innocent procedure were not lost on the Athenians. The craftsmen, said Socrates, had their own expertise, but were at a loss when it came to an understanding of the large and important conceptions of ethics or politics. Athenian democracy, on the other hand, was based on just the opposite assumption, namely that all citizens alike, whatever their daily occupation, were equally well qualified to deal with questions of public policy, which was not a matter of any special skill. As Socrates expresses it in the *Protagoras* (319D), in professional matters the Athenian assembly demands expert advice, but in business connected with the policy of the State it is ready to listen to anyone – smith, shoemaker, merchant, sea-captain, rich or poor, of good family or none. To Socrates the successful pursuit of any occupation demanded the mastery of a particular knowledge, skill, or technique; and this was above all true of the direction of the city's affairs, on which questions of peace and war, and the whole happiness of the citizens, necessarily depended. By his criterion Athenian democracy stood condemned.

Socrates then, who started out, as he claimed, in all humility to learn from others, decided in the end that, whereas he and they alike knew nothing, he was to this extent superior, that he was aware of his own ignorance. And since no one will try to find out what constitutes right action, or what is the real meaning of freedom or justice, if he thinks he knows it already, the first task was to convince others too of their ignorance. Then together they could start the inquiry with some hope of success.

This endeavour to show people that they knew nothing goes far to explain why Socrates shared the odium with which conservative Athenian opinion regarded the Sophists, but we can see the essential difference between them. They believed the kind of knowledge he sought to be impossible, because absolute and universal moral qualities did not exist to be known. When they claimed to teach virtue they had nothing of that sort in mind, but only a purely practical and empirical training. His procedure on the other hand was based on a passionate conviction that the knowledge could be attained, and moreover that the only way to reform conduct was to lead men to an understanding of certain permanent and unvarying principles on which to base it; but his conversations had shown him that most men suffered from an illusion of knowledge which must be dispelled before the positive side of the inquiry could begin. The two sides of the process are clearly demonstrated in the *Meno*, where at the end of the first stage Meno complains bitterly of the sense of frustration and mental incapacity to which Socrates's questions have reduced him.

His method then was to put the dilemma: Is there such a thing as (e.g.) justice, or not? If not, why keep talking about it? If so, what is it? What is there in common between all actions called just, that makes men give them that name? He rejects the faulty definitions that are first offered, and by going deeper and considering a wider range of examples, tries to lead on to one which will adequately describe the concept under consideration. 'Justice, you say, is giving to every man what belongs to him: Suppose I have a dagger belonging to a homicidal maniac: is it justice to return it to him?' And so on. Recent history and his own extraordinary character made it so natural for Socrates to link together the ideas of intellectual ignorance or scepticism and moral imperfection that he sincerely, if somewhat naïvely, believed that this clearing of the mind alone was required to bring about moral reformation: if men understood the true nature of what was good (no small demand, for it meant no less than a knowledge of the true end and aim of human life) they would inevitably seek it. Hence his famous paradoxes: 'Virtue is knowledge' and 'No one does wrong willingly.'

That is the contribution of Socrates. He did not think he had himself attained this knowledge, but he was convinced that right and wrong and similar notions were not just a matter of the expediency of the moment, changing with the changing needs of individual or state, but permanent and universal principles with a nature of their own. In method also he differed from the Sophists, for in his view the kind of knowledge needed was not to be imparted in public lectures, but could only be attained by two or three people, all convinced of their own ignorance, trying to hammer out the truth together in informal conversation ('dialectic' in the Socratic sense) and in a spirit of mutual helpfulness.

Socrates was no metaphysician, and went no further than his practical and ethical aims required.* But when, after his execution, Plato wished to carry on the battle for the same ideals, he found that Socrates had bequeathed to him a whole complex of problems concerned both with the possibility of knowledge and with the nature of reality. Implicit in the demand for definitions was the assumption that justice, courage, virtue or whatever it was, is a *thing* which *exists*; for what would be the point of trying to define something which has no existence? But is there in fact such a thing as absolute justice or virtue, apart from the individual actions which we call just or good? No one would claim that any of these is 'justice itself'; they are all thought of as only imperfect instances of, or approximations to, it. What then, and where, is this justice or

* The question where the thought of Socrates ends and that of Plato begins (the 'Socratic question') is a famous subject of academic controversy. It could scarcely be otherwise, seeing that Socrates wrote nothing himself and the words that he is made to utter in Plato's dialogues are our most important (though not our sole) source for his ideas. A writer can only give his own view, which in this case agrees with the testimony of Aristotle and would probably command a wide measure of assent today.

virtue? It is not in this world. And if, as Plato did, we reply that nevertheless it does exist, laid up as a pattern for earthly action in a world beyond space and time, we have then to face the further question how we can ever come to have knowledge of it, since we do not experience it on this earth. Plato's answers to these further questions, almost certainly not raised by Socrates yet arising directly out of his teaching, do not concern us as we read the *Protagoras*, but begin to make their appearance in the *Meno*. They lead to new, and perhaps at first sight incongruous, regions of thought. On the one hand, in investigating the possibility of eternal and changeless moral truths, it seemed to Plato natural and helpful to link it to another science in which the existence of timeless truth is universally acknowledged – the science of mathematics; and on the other hand the attempt to discover a connection between these timeless entities and our own powers of cognition led him to assert the immortality and reincarnation of the human soul, for only in another world could we have acquired the knowledge of something which can never be presented to us in the course of earthly experience.

The *Protagoras* raises no metaphysical questions. It is innocent of those doctrines which we think of as distinctively Platonic, the doctrine that asserts the existence of transcendent forms (the 'Ideas') and the theory of learning as the recollection of knowledge acquired in a pre-natal state and dormant in us since birth. It remains on the everyday, practical level generally associated with the name of Socrates. It ends, like the *Meno*, with the suggestion that the reason for the failure of Socrates and Protagoras to find a satisfactory answer to the question whether virtue can be taught must be that they ought to have inquired first what in fact virtue *is*. This however is as much a Socratic as a Platonic question, and the dialogue has contained no hint of the theory of knowledge as recollection which plays an important part in the *Meno*, where it is carefully explained and demonstrated as if Plato were introducing his readers to it for the first time. In reading the *Protagoras* one almost gets the impression that it might be the actual record of a conversation which took place between Socrates and the Sophists a few years before Plato was born – the time in which the dialogue is dramatically set.

Since it is fairly certain that Plato did not write anything until after Socrates's death, this raises its own problems. Was Plato in fact aiming only at a historical reconstruction of the kind of arguments that Socrates and the Sophists used to have? Was it that he did not consider his own special doctrines of Ideas and of reincarnation to be relevant to the discussion of a practical subject like the acquisition of political and private *savoir vivre*? Instances could be quoted of the deliberate omission of these beliefs in dialogues which must be supposed on other grounds to have been written after they had become a part of his philosophy. On the other hand they evidently seemed indispensable in a discussion of exactly the same topic in the *Meno*. This inclines us to the other possibility, namely that the *Protagoras* was written earlier, before Plato himself had thought out these doctrines and seen in them, as he came to do, the only way of providing a solid and reasoned defence of his master's paradox that 'virtue is knowledge'.

There is one feature of the *Protagoras* which cannot fail to puzzle, if not exasperate, a reader: the behaviour of Socrates. At times he treats the discussion with such levity, and at other times with such unscrupulousness, that Wilamowitz felt bound to conclude that the dialogue could only have been written in his lifetime. This, he wrote, is the human being whom Plato knew; only after he had suffered a martyr's death did the need assert itself to idealize his character. This mischievousness of Socrates is not only seen in his exposition of the poem of Simonides (342A–347A), a brilliant parody of a particular type of Sophist's lecture which we may surely enjoy without troubling our conscience too much on Socrates's behalf. Both before and after his outrageous distortions of the poem, we are given

18

clear warning what to expect. Socrates has tried to keep the discussion on his own lines of question and answer, but this has led to a breakdown. Now it is the Sophist's turn, and we are due for a display of his chosen method of continuous exposition, in which Socrates explicitly avows his disbelief. Since Plato's aim to show up its inadequacy, he sees no harm in further enlivening this entertaining work by treating it in a vein of broad humour. Ostensibly Protagoras has agreed to continue by the method of question and answer, but we know that that is not what he wants, nor is it what we get. It is the turn for Sophistry, and Socrates himself tacitly adopts the procedure of a Sophist, launching out into a long, continuous exhibition of virtuosity. Since this is what the assembled Sophists most admire, it does not occur to any of them to protest at his failure to keep the bargain which he himself has suggested. When he has finished, he lets us know what to think of his effort by putting all talk about poetry on a level with watching a cabaret turn after a good dinner! (347c). Few things in the dialogue are better than his solemn description of the Spartans as the most philosophical of the Greeks, whose apparent lack of interest in culture, and addiction to the more brutal physical sports, is an elaborate disguise. The motive for their periodical expulsions of foreigners is to have the opportunity to indulge in a secret orgy of philosophical discussion.

More serious are several instances of palpably fallacious or unfair argument. These either pass undetected or else (as at 350c) stir Protagoras to a mild protest. When this happens, Socrates makes no attempt to defend himself, but simply lets the argument drop and starts a new one. All this must be seen in the setting of the whole dialogue, and more especially related to the argument at the end in which Socrates comes out as the champion of a form of hedonism (the equation of the concepts 'good' and 'pleasant'), in a curiously roundabout way it is true, but nevertheless with no sign that he does not himself approve of what he is saying. This too has caused bewilderment, and a variety of theories to explain it.

I would suggest that the clue is to be found in the formal side of the dialogue, the choice of characters and the atmosphere (clearly created with great care, and attention to the minutest details) in which the discussion is carried on. The subject is virtue, and Socrates attempts to maintain his favourite thesis that all the so-called virtues are reducible to one, and this one thing is knowledge. But on the other hand he is not, as in some other dialogues, talking to a docile and co-operative young friend, but to the greatest of the Sophists, a man who, as he says himself (317C), could so far as years go be the father of any of those present. Socrates knows that however well he argues, he will never convert this man to his point of view. It is no use trying to treat him like one of the intimate circle of disciples who share his ideal of the 'common search'. Protagoras is a successful philosopher in his own right, his reputation is established and his views have hardened. This gives the dialogue a superficial incoherence. When one line of argument has been carried a certain distance the incompatibility of outlook becomes too obvious, the thread must simply be dropped and a new one picked up. Every now and then the friendly intervention of the listeners is necessary to prevent the discussion breaking down altogether.

On the other hand a feature of the conversation which cannot fail to strike a reader is its unbroken urbanity and good temper. The keynote is courtesy and forbearance, though these are not always forthcoming without a struggle. Socrates is constantly on the alert for signs of displeasure on the part of Protagoras, and when he detects them, is careful not to press his point, and the dialogue ends with mutual expressions of esteem. Nor can one doubt after reading this work that Plato had a high opinion of Protagoras both as a thinker and as a moral influence. He disagreed profoundly with the basic assumptions of his thought, and his satirical sense of humour did not miss the opportunities afforded by the Sophist's inflated opinion of his own good qualities. But the admiration was there. Protagoras had a fine mind, his thoughts went deeper than those of the other Sophists, and although he might deal in relatives where Socrates and Plato sought for absolutes, his moral teaching was far from reprehensible. Socrates may laugh at his vanity, but time and again it is Protagoras who is made to argue both ably and attractively where Socrates, we feel, is being inconsiderate or unfair.

We may contrast another dialogue in which Socrates is faced with the arguments of Sophistry – the *Gorgias*. There his opponent Callicles adopts the most extreme and unpleasing of the Sophists' interpretations of their common assumption that law and custom are man-made and mutable. Since law and morality are matters of convention and agreement, he says, they are contrary to nature, and the proper aim of life is to follow nature. If therefore a man has it in his nature to outgrow the pettiness of conventional morality and put himself above the law, it is his natural right, indeed his duty, to acquire domination and use it solely for his personal gratification. As one might expect, the tone of the conversation becomes bitter and ill-tempered. Socrates does express his own convictions fully, though here too he is talking not to a disciple but to an out-and-out opponent whom he cannot hope to convert. Rather, when Callicles has expressed his point of view forcibly and even abusively, Socrates in his turn gets angry. He practically pins Callicles in a corner and says: 'All right, you have had your say. Now it's my turn. You may not believe me, but that will not prevent me from telling you that unless you recognize the truth, which is the exact opposite of what you at present believe, you have a bad time coming to you.'

All this is quite alien to the mutual tolerance, the friendly banter, the politeness of the *Protagoras*. Protagoras, though he shares the general Sophistic belief that law and morality are the product of convention, is nevertheless their champion. He too claimed that knowledge or wisdom was the highest thing in life (352C,D), and would repudiate as scornfully as Socrates the almost bestial type of hedonism advocated by Callicles, who says that what nature means by fair and right is for the strong man to let his desires grow as big as possible and have the means of everlastingly satisfying them. The doctrine to which Socrates obtains Protagoras's consent towards the end of the dialogue may be labelled hedonism, but it is something utterly different from this, and is indeed consistent with a morality as high as most people would aspire to. Among its demands, after all, are the living of a temperate life in the interests of health and strength, and the endurance of pain and hardship whenever these may be necessary for the safety of one's country (354B). This is hardly hedonism in any accepted sense.

The natural conclusion from a reading of the dialogue is that Plato is not making Socrates deliberately mislead Protagoras – whom he regards with genuine admiration and liking – nor is he putting before him the Socratic view of virtue in its full paradoxical rigour. This would be no use, and Socrates is not tempted by Protagoras, as he is by the very different outlook and manners of a Callicles, to ram it down his throat whether he can take it or not. What he does is to carry his arguments to the furthest point at which a Sophist can accept them. He employs the Sophists' own premises, that all moral values are relative and there are no criteria of action other than empiricism and expediency. No doubt he draws from these premises consequences which had not been perceived by any actual Sophist, but he does not go further and challenge the premises themselves. Thus he can take them with him at every step. And he does this not (as he sometimes does elsewhere and has been thought by many to be doing here) in order simply to refute them or reveal their inadequacy, but in a genuine attempt to put their opinions in the most favourable light. The result, considered as an exposition of Socraticism, is curiously incomplete. What Plato has achieved is something different. By confronting Socrates, in the friendly atmosphere of a house at which they are both guests, with the best and most likeable of the Sophists, he has indicated fairly and temperately both how near the best of the Sophists could come to the wisdom of Socrates and how far he fell short of it.

It is after all a sound procedure, if you wish to oppose a position, to make yourself see it first in the best light possible. Nor did Plato need to fear that by stopping short, in the present encounter with Protagoras, of the full teaching of Socrates, he was casting any doubt on what that teaching was. He was to make that clear in many other dialogues, including the *Meno*. Even if, as is very possible, the historic Socrates went no further than to raise the concept of 'the advantageous' to the level of a universal ideal (*Meno* 87E), the quest for it gave him an entirely different outlook even from that of a hedonism carried to the almost unrecognizable degree of refinement which we find in the *Protagoras*. The quest for knowledge of this universal good meant (as he says in the *Apology*) that he must renounce the claims not only of immediate enjoyment but also of health, livelihood, the service of his country in public business, and finally life itself. To the Sophists in the *Protagoras* he argues that, even on the popular estimate of what constitutes good living, knowledge is necessary for its attainment. But in the *Phaedo* Plato scarcely goes beyond the historic Socrates when he contrasts the ideal of the *philosophos*, the disinterested seeker after wisdom, alike with that of the lovers of material goods and the lovers of honour. It is in the ranks of the latter that the Sophists and their pupils were to be found, and that is a measure of the difference between the 'virtue' of which they were the professed teachers, and that advocated by Socrates.

Enough, I hope, has been said to show that the superficially unsatisfactory features of the *Protagoras* – the occasional incoherence of the argument, the false starts and abrupt transitions, the fallacies and trivialities – irritating though they may still be to a modern reader, yet have their place in an artistically constructed whole. They are part of its dramatic realism, and this in its turn serves the philosophic purpose of showing what happens when Socraticism and Sophistry meet in friendly – not acrimonious – discussion. The *Protagoras* is the perfect foil to the *Meno*, in which the same questions – Is virtue teachable? Is it a unity or a plurality? What is it anyway? – are discussed again, this time continuously and seriously. For most of the dialogue Socrates and Meno are the only participants. Meno does not behave like a proud and temperamental Sophist, and Socrates does not allow himself the levities and trivialities with which he tries the patience of Protagoras. The *Meno* is one of the most interesting of Plato's dialogues, and the best of all to serve as an introduction to the study of his thought. The reason for this has been touched on already, and since the dialogue is here to speak for itself, there is no need to say much more. Plato's starting point was his intense admiration for the personality and teaching of Socrates, and in the majority of his dialogues Socrates is the chief speaker. Obviously much of what he has to say was inherent in Socrates's own conversations, but it is equally obvious that Plato was no mere follower but an original thinker in his own right. On the vexed question where Socrates ends and Plato begins, there is nowadays a growing measure of agreement, and probably few scholars would quarrel with the statement that in the *Meno* one can see the transition taking place. It shows the mind of Plato assimilating what Socrates had to give and then, under other, particularly Pythagorean influences, as well as the individual bent of his own temperament, reaching out beyond it to regions of which Socrates scarcely dreamed. It was the Pythagoreans who introduced him to the timeless world of mathematics, and they too who held the religious doctrine of reincarnation in which he saw a solution to the problem of knowledge. If the practical temperament of Socrates was less open to this kind of speculation, we need not on that account feel surprise that Plato should have put it into his mouth, for he saw in it no contradiction but only a natural extension of his master's teaching and indeed the only possible defence against the attacks to which it was exposed. It is hardly going too far to say that one can put one's finger on the actual place in the *Meno* where the transition occurs, in the passage (81A) where the tone of Socrates's utterance suddenly seems to change and become more solemn as he introduces the doctrine of 'certain priests and priestesses and many of the inspired poets'.

The dates of composition of the two dialogues cannot be fixed with certainty, but we have seen reason for thinking that the *Meno* is a somewhat later work than the *Protagoras*. The interval need not have been long, but probably included Plato's first visit to the Greek colonies of Italy and Sicily, which gave him the friendship of the mathematician and Pythagorean philosopher Archytas of Tarentum and quickened his interest in Pythagorean doctrine. This visit took place about 387 B.C., when Plato was forty and we shall not go far wrong if we put the *Protagoras* in the 390s and the *Meno* not long after 387.

It only remains to add something which should cause no surprise after what has already been said about the general character of the Platonic dialogues, namely that they are open to a number of different interpretations. This applies particularly to the discussion of hedonism in the *Protagoras*. The explanation of this which has been given here does not coincide exactly with any other views, and the reader may find it interesting, when he has finished the dialogue, to decide for himself how far he thinks it is true.

My thanks are due to Professor R. Hackforth, who has read this translation in proof and is responsible for a number of improvements.

W.K.C.G.

THE PROTAGORAS

DRAMATIC DATE

THE date at which the conversation is supposed to take place is in the late 430s. Pericles is still in power at Athens, and his sons (who were to die in the plague of 429) are still alive. The Peloponnesian War has not yet broken out, Alcibiades is a young man 'with his first beard' and the tragic poet Agathon is a mere boy. Socrates is perhaps thirty-six. The reference (at 327D) to a play of Pherecrates which is known to have been produced in 420 must be accepted as an anachronism of the incidental kind which Plato took no particular pains to avoid.

SPEAKERS IN THE DIALOGUE

Socrates.

Hippocrates son of Apollodorus. An impetuous and ambitious young friend of Socrates, known only from this dialogue.

Callias son of Hipponicus, well known as the richest man in Athens. Comic poets describe him as extravagant and dissolute, but he had a taste for culture which made him a gold-mine for the Sophists. Here he keeps open house for them, in the *Cratylus* he is said to have spent much money on them, and in the *Apology* Socrates calls him the man 'who has paid more to the Sophists than all the others together'. He had family connections with the highest political circles, for after the death of his father Hipponicus his mother married Pericles, so that we find one of Pericles's sons described as Callias's half-brother. Besides his house in Athens, he had another in the Piraeus, where the scene of Xenophon's *Symposium* is laid.

27

Protagoras of Abdera. A Sophist, i.e. a professional teacher
who made a large fortune by lecture-tours and public
displays of his knowledge. He was, however, head and
shoulders above other Sophists both in intellectual
powers and in moral worth. He was the author of the
saying: 'Man is the measure of all things, of those that
are that they are, and of those that are not that they are
not.' The natural meaning of this is what Plato took it
to be, that knowledge is relative to the knower, and that
therefore no man can call another wrong. I say it is colder
today, you say it is warmer. Then for me it is colder, and
for you it is warmer, and there is no more to be said. We
cannot profitably argue the point. Also famous was his
confession of religious agnosticism: 'Concerning the
gods I cannot say either that they exist or that they do
not, or what they are like in form; for there are many
hindrances to knowledge: the obscurity of the subject
and the brevity of human life.' Plato, though disagreeing
profoundly with his scepticism, always treats his views
with respect, and we may take it that what is attributed
to him in our dialogue (like the interesting theory of
knowledge with which he is credited in the *Theaetetus*)
is a fair representation of his views. He died about 420
at the age of seventy.

Hippias of Elis. Another Sophist, of whom a lively portrait
is given in two other dialogues of Plato named after him.
He was a polymath, who claimed proficiency not only in
theoretical studies like mathematics, astronomy, and
grammar, but also in the practical arts, and was said to
have appeared at the Olympic festival wearing nothing
that he had not made himself. The antithesis between
nature and convention, attributed to him at 337 C-D, was
a favourite theme of the Sophists.

Prodicus of Ceos. For some reason Socrates was fond of
referring to himself humorously as a pupil and admirer of
this Sophist. This may well be because his speciality was
the right use of words and the careful discrimination

between apparent synonyms. Since Socrates believed that an accurate understanding of terms, and their correct definition, would have momentous results in the sphere of conduct, it is likely enough that he attended a lecture of Prodicus with high hopes. The discovery of the pedantic and hair-splitting nature of the Sophist's distinctions would then account for the irony that creeps into Socrates's tributes.

Alcibiades. Little need be said here about this brilliant and wayward star of Athenian life. His relations with Socrates are fully dealt with in the *Symposium*, where Plato is at pains to demonstrate that the behaviour which contributed so much towards the downfall of Athens sprang from his inherent defects of character, and was not the result of any 'corruption' by Socrates as the accusers of Socrates maintained.

Critias. A relation of Plato's on his mother's side, who earned an infamous name as the most violent of all the 'Thirty Tyrants' of 404. In earlier life he had been an associate of Socrates, but also of the Sophists to whom his mind was more akin. He wrote elegiac poems and tragedies, one of which contains a purely non-religious account of the origins of society, and the assertion that the gods are a clever invention to keep men from misbehaving when no one is watching them.

FOR reasons which have been explained in the introduction, the argument of the *Protagoras* is disjointed and cannot easily be reduced to summary form, but the following attempt may be of some assistance to the reader.

A young friend Hippocrates rouses Socrates before it is light in his eagerness to be introduced to the great Sophist Protagoras, who is on a visit to Athens. Since it is too early to visit him, Socrates passes the time by questioning Hippocrates on his motives and making him confess his ignorance of the true nature of the Sophist's art. This introductory scene ensures that we to go meet the Sophists in a mood very different from that of uncritical admiration with which they are surrounded at the house of their patron. Socrates has put certain questions, and certain suspicions, in our minds. What is this wisdom that they profess to impart? Is it a good or a bad thing? Do they even know themselves which it is? Have they indeed got anything that they can impart at all? It is a challenge to the whole Sophistic philosophy of life, which Socrates is clearly ready to present to them face to face.

After a description of the scene at Callias's house, and the galaxy of talent assembled there, Socrates tells how he introduced Hippocrates to Protagoras, who gives a little disquisition on his own conception of the Sophist's art. A circle is formed to listen to the talk, and Socrates begins by asking what kind of benefit Hippocrates may expect to receive from Protagoras's teaching. He will, says Protagoras, acquire *arete*, which he defines as the ability to be successful both in private and public life. Socrates expresses his doubt whether this is a possible subject of teaching; at any rate, he says, the affairs of Athens do not seem to be conducted on that assumption. On subjects which can be learned such as architecture or shipbuilding, the Assembly will not listen to the counsel of any but experts, yet on political questions they demand no credentials but give every citizen an equal right to speak. Moreover, men pre-eminent in this kind of excellence do not seem to instruct their sons in it. Otherwise the sons of great men would not turn out failures, as they so often do.

Protagoras replies in a long and brilliant speech which, one must admit, meets Socrates's points without evasion. He begins with a mythical account of the origins of society which is either an extract from the Sophist's actual work or a close imitation. The selfconsciously poetic diction and artificial balance of phrase are far removed from Plato's normal style. In spite of its mythical form, it is a serious exposition of an evolutionary view which can be partly matched in earlier Ionian thought, and is doubtless sub-stantially that of the lost work on the foundations of society which Protagoras is known to have written. Moral and political wisdom, he says, were not, like technical ability, human perquisites in the beginning, but were acquired later because they proved to be necessary for common action, and failure to combine threatened our whole race with the prospect of being destroyed by its more powerful enemies in the animal world. In men as they now are, there-fore, *arete* is (a) universal, but (b) not an essential and original part of human nature. Men differ in the degree to which they possess it, but a man devoid of this quality is unlikely to be found, and if he were, would have to be put to death as unworthy of belonging to the human race. Point (a) justifies the Athenian belief that anyone may have something worth while to say on questions of moral and political conduct, since in comparison with those who lived in the primitive age before the race acquired its moral sense, everyone may claim to possess it; point (b) however (the general Sophistic tenet that virtue is not 'by nature') means that everyone is capable of being improved. That the Athenians do combine this belief with the other is shown by their use of reprimand, correction, and punish-ment, the aim of which can only be remedial and educative.

Why then do good men not see that their sons are taught virtue? The answer is a denial of the fact: they do. At home children receive moral admonition and instruction, and again at school the primary aim of education is moral. After school age the State continues the process. The laws are patterns for right living, to which the citizen is taught to conform by the punishment which follows transgression. Since virtue, unlike the special techniques, is something which *no one* must be without if human beings are to live together at all, everyone – parents, school, State, neighbours, and friends – is a teacher of it and imparts it to others in different degrees.

But why do the sons of good men so often turn out bad? Simply because there are differences in natural aptitude for goodness. The objection of Socrates implies that these young men have no goodness (*arete*) in them at all, as e.g. the son of a good musician might be unable to play a note. But this is not so. To make the parallel valid, one would have to suppose that a certain minimum competence in playing was a necessity of life in communities. In that case, everyone would have to play after a fashion, and one would not expect the son of a good player always to outshine his contemporaries: it would depend on whether he had the same natural talent as his father. So it is in our cities with virtue: men considered wicked in Athens are not absolutely so. If you could really meet with a man completely lacking in virtue – who *ex hypothesi* would be leading a solitary, brutish life and in any civilized community would be put to death without hesitation – you would long for the villains of Athens as being, by comparison, paragons of virtue. Everyone has some virtue, and he has got it through teaching which started in babyhood and continues throughout life. To ask who are the teachers of it is like asking who taught you to speak your native language.

Has not Protagoras then destroyed his claim to set up as a professional teacher of the good life? Well, he says, though everyone teaches it to some extent, naturally some are better at this than others. As it happens, I honestly believe that I can teach it better than anyone else. That is my case.

In the next section Socrates takes the lead, and it must be admitted that he tries the sympathy and patience of a reader by apparently going about the business at inordinate length, sometimes merely playing with words, and sometimes being allowed to get away with what are to us elementary fallacies. It is important to be aware of his purpose, which remains constant throughout the dialogue, though often obscured by the indirectness of his approach and the thickets of verbiage and quibbling argument in which it is concealed. A reading of the *Meno* is helpful at this point, for the same purpose is there pursued more openly and clearly. A specific question about virtue, like 'Can it be taught?', ought not, in his view, to be asked until we have determined its essential nature. The definition must come first. Through all the trivialities of his argument, he retains at the back of his mind the conviction (upheld at *Meno* 87C–89A) that all virtue is essentially one, being reducible to wisdom or knowledge, and it is this that he wishes Protagoras to understand and admit.

He begins by raising the question of what a Greek called separate virtues – justice, courage, temperance, holiness, wisdom – and their relation to the single whole concept virtue. Are they parts of it, differing from one another like the features of a face, or are they just different aspects of (or as he puts it more forcibly, different names for) the same thing, virtue? The latter of course is his own view: in every case it is the element of understanding which constitutes the good and is therefore the essential virtue in the so-called 'virtue' – distinguishing courage from foolhardiness, temperance from pointless or harmful austerity and so on.

First he tries, by questionable means, to make Protagoras admit that the pair justice and holiness at least resemble one another, on the grounds that otherwise holiness will be unjust. When Protagoras demurs, this line is dropped and in a new argument Socrates tries to prove the identity of another pair, wisdom and temperance. After getting Protagoras to agree that one thing can have only one contrary, he then traps him into saying that folly is the contrary of both. Without pause (except for an exhortation to Protagoras not to grow weary) he passes to another line of attack. This time the pair of virtues to be proved identical are justice and temperance, which, on the very doubtful assumption that the truth of his previous contentions can now be admitted, would establish the identity of all four. The present argument requires the admission that it is possible to act 'temperately' (or 'sensibly'; the Greek word is difficult to render exactly) when committing an injustice. Protagoras is unwilling to agree to this, though admitting that many people believe it. With some difficulty, Socrates persuades him to answer for the others rather than for himself. But the atmosphere is becoming unhappy. The introduction of the ambiguous Greek phrase which means both to 'fare well' and to 'do well' leads Socrates to ask Protagoras what he understands by the word 'good'. This gives Protagoras, who has been growing increasingly restive, the opportunity to escape from the rain of questions by launching into a short and able harangue on his favourite theory of the relativity of goodness. His speech brings on a disruption of the argument and a quarrel which threatens to break up the meeting. Others intervene and a long interlude ensues.

Eventually Protagoras agrees to continue the procedure of question and answer with himself in the lead. He will transfer the discussion to the realm of poetry, taking a poem of Simonides on their chosen topic of virtue and questioning Socrates as to its meaning. The interpretation of poetry, the didactic import of which was universally accepted in Greece, was a common vehicle of Sophistic instruction, and the upshot is a long parody of such instruction by Socrates, in which he shamelessly misconstrues

Simonides and wins the approval of Hippias. This entertaining digression does not further the main argument in the slightest, and at the end of it Socrates makes an earnest plea for his own method of the 'common search', carried out not by alternate bursts of competitive eloquence but by 'two going together', each helping the other to the best of his ability.

Once more granted the lead, he goes back to the question of the identity of the virtues. Taking the example of courage, he pursues a niggling and in parts fallacious argument, the kernel of which is that men may be bold or confident *either* as a result of knowledge *or* as a result of ignorance. Only the former are called brave. Hence what turns boldness, or rashness, into courage is knowledge. His aim is, by proving courage to be knowledge, to take the most difficult step towards substantiating his main conviction that virtue as a whole is knowledge. Protagoras objects that the conclusion has only been reached by illegitimately converting his statement that the courageous are confident into a statement that all who are confident are courageous. It is doubtful whether Socrates really intended to do this, but in any case the two have got themselves into a rare state of confusion, and seeing no way out of it, Socrates once more gives up and makes a fresh start.

His final attempt to get Protagoras to admit that virtue is knowledge is the famous 'defence of hedonism'. Does not Protagoras agree that what is pleasant, *qua* pleasant, in isolation from its consequences, is *ipso facto* good? Protagoras is doubtful, but agrees to investigate the question. Socrates starts the inquiry by getting Protagoras's willing agreement to the view (which was of course his own) that knowledge is the ruling element in life. Most men think otherwise. They believe that a man may do evil with full knowledge, because he has been mastered by a desire for pleasure, i.e. his knowledge does not govern his actions but is at the mercy of his impulses. He and Protagoras, however, know better, and he goes on, in both their names, to prove to 'the many' that they are wrong, and that, on admissions which they themselves would make, such behaviour can only be made possible by an element of ignorance about its full consequences. When the many speak of succumbing to pleasure as an evil, they really mean choosing an immediately pleasant course although it will bring pain – in the shape of poverty, disease or suchlike – in its train; and conversely by choosing a painful course which is good, they mean one that will lead to greater pleasure in the future, or at least an avoidance of greater pains, because it will win for them health or riches, or mean the difference between subjection to others and freedom or domination.

Once granted that, if it were pointed out to them, the many would be bound to see that all this is implicit in their philosophy of life, it is easy for Socrates to go on to show that, on the assumption attributed to them, all they need to attain their ideal is the ability to weigh and measure pleasures and pains against each other. This is a science, and it is only the lack of that science which can account for a man being, as they would put it, seduced by pleasure into taking a wrong course.

So far, it seems only to be agreed that this is the logical outcome of accepting the views of 'the many' on what constitutes right living. At the end, however, by putting it in the general form that to live the good life on this basis calls for knowledge, and reminding the assembled Sophists that this is exactly what they themselves provide (so that it is an excellent advertisement for their calling), Socrates traps them all into agreeing enthusiastically that it is their view too.

With so much agreed, Socrates returns to his abandoned thesis that the individual virtue of courage is identical with knowledge. While ready to admit the identity, or at least similarity, of all the other virtues, Protagoras has hitherto maintained that courage is something quite separate. Since the identity of good and pleasant is now agreed, and we may no longer speak of a man's succumbing to pleasure against his better judgement, it follows that no one will voluntarily choose a worse course instead of a better, since that would be to choose the less pleasant. If he does choose the worse, it can only be through ignorance that the other was better. Now fear is the expectation of evil, so if no one goes voluntarily to meet what he knows or believes to be evil, no one (whether brave man or coward) goes to meet what he believes to be fearful. It is true that brave men go willingly to battle, and cowards do not; but the only explanation we can now admit is that the brave know that to enter battle is both better and pleasanter than to run away, and the cowards are ignorant of this. Thus the thesis is proved, that courage is knowledge.

In conclusion, Socrates remarks that it is curious how he and Protagoras seem to have changed places. Protagoras, who claims that virtue can be taught, is reluctant to admit that it can be knowledge, whereas Socrates, who was sceptical about the possibility of teaching it, is doing his best to prove that it is knowledge. Yet what can be taught if not knowledge? No doubt, he says, the reason for their confusion is that they have put the cart before the horse by trying to settle a particular question about virtue, to discuss whether or not it has a particular characteristic, before agreeing on its general definition.

THE PROTAGORAS

Socrates meets an unnamed friend.

309A   FRIEND. Where have you come from, Socrates? No doubt
from pursuit of the captivating Alcibiades. Certainly
when I saw him only a day or two ago, he seemed to be
still a handsome man; but between ourselves, Socrates,
'man' is the word. He's actually growing a beard.

SOCRATES. What of it? Aren't you an enthusiast for
B   Homer, who says that the most charming age is that of
the youth with his first beard, just the age of Alcibiades
now?

FRIEND. Well what's the news? Have you just left the
young man, and how is he disposed towards you?

SOCRATES. Very well, I think, particularly today, since he
came to my assistance and spoke up for me at some
length. For as you guessed, I have only just left him.
But I will tell you a surprising thing: although he was
present, I had no thought for him, and often forgot
him altogether.

C   FRIEND. Why, what can have happened between you and
him to make such a difference? You surely can't have
met someone more handsome – not in Athens at least?

SOCRATES. Yes, much more.

FRIEND. Really? An Athenian or a foreigner?

SOCRATES. A foreigner.

FRIEND. Where from?

SOCRATES. Abdera.

FRIEND. And this stranger struck you as such a handsome
person that you put him above the son of Clinias in that
respect?

SOCRATES. Yes. Must not perfect wisdom take the palm
for handsomeness?

FRIEND. You mean you have just been meeting some wise man?

SOCRATES. Say rather the wisest man now living, if you D agree that that description fits Protagoras.

FRIEND. What? Protagoras is in Athens?

SOCRATES. And has been for two days.

FRIEND. And you have just now come from seeing him?

SOCRATES. Yes, we had a long talk together. 310

FRIEND. Then lose no time in telling me about your conversation, if you are free. Sit down here; the slave will make room for you.

SOCRATES. Certainly I shall, and be grateful to you for listening.

FRIEND. And I to you for your story.

SOCRATES. That means a favour on both sides. Listen then.

Last night, a little before daybreak, Hippocrates son of Apollodorus, Phason's brother, knocked violently on my door with his stick, and when it was opened, came straight B in in a great hurry and shouted out:

'Socrates, are you awake or asleep?' I recognized his voice and said:

'That will be Hippocrates. No bad news I hope?'

'Nothing but good' he replied.

'I'm glad to hear it' said I. 'What is it then, and what brings you here at such an hour?'

'Protagoras has arrived' he said, taking his stand beside me.

'The day before yesterday. Have you only just found out?'

'Only last evening.' As he said this he felt for the bed C and sat by my feet, adding: 'Yes, yesterday evening, when I got back late from Oenoe. My slave Satyrus had run away from me. I meant to let you know that I was going after him, but something put it out of my head. When I got back and we had had dinner and were just going to bed, my

brother mentioned to me that Protagoras had come. Late
D as it was, I nearly came to see you straight away, then I
decided it was really too far into the night; but as soon as
I had slept off my tiredness, I got up at once and came
here as you see.'

I recognized his determination and the state of excite-
ment he was in, and asked him: 'What is your concern in
this? Has Protagoras done you any harm?'

'Of course he has, Socrates' replied Hippocrates laughing. 'He keeps his wisdom to himself instead of sharing it
with me.'

'Not at all' said I. 'If you pay him sufficient to persuade
him, he will make you wise too.'

E 'If it were only a question of that!' he said despairingly.
'I shouldn't keep back a penny of my own money, or my
friends' money either. But this is just the reason why I
have come to you, to persuade you to speak to him on my
behalf. For one thing I am too young, and for another I
have never seen nor heard Protagoras. Last time he came
to Athens I was still a child. But you know, Socrates, everyone is singing his praises and saying that he is the cleverest
of speakers. Do let's pay him a visit at once, to make sure
311 of finding him in. He's staying, so I'm told, with Callias
son of Hipponicus. Come on.'

'My dear Hippocrates' I said, 'we can't go there at this
early hour. Let's come out here into the courtyard and walk
around it to pass the time until it gets light. Then we can
go. Protagoras spends most of his time indoors, so don't
worry; we are pretty sure to catch him there.'

So then we got up and walked about in the courtyard,
B and to try Hippocrates's mettle I began to examine and
question him. 'Tell me this, Hippocrates' I said. 'It is
your present intention to go to Protagoras and pay him
money as a fee on your behalf. Now whom do you think
you are going to, and what will he make of you? Suppose
for instance you had it in mind to go to your namesake
Hippocrates of Cos, the doctor, and pay him a fee on your

own behalf, and someone asked you in what capacity you C
thought of Hippocrates with the intention of paying him,
what would you answer?'

'I should say, in his capacity as a doctor.'

'And what would you hope to become?'

'A doctor.'

'And suppose your idea was to go to Polyclitus of
Argos or Phidias of Athens and pay them fees for your
own benefit, and someone asked you in what capacity you
thought of paying this money to them, what would you
answer?'

'I should say, in their capacity as sculptors.'

'To make you what?'

'A sculptor, obviously.'

'Right' said I. 'Now here are you and I going to Pro- D
tagoras prepared to pay him money as a fee for you – our
own if it is enough to satisfy him, or if not, our friends'
resources thrown in as well. If then, seeing us so full of
enthusiasm, someone should ask: "Tell me, Socrates and
Hippocrates, what do you suppose Protagoras is, that you
intend to pay him money?" what should we answer him?
What particular name do we hear attached to Protagoras in E
the sort of way that Phidias is called a sculptor and Homer
a poet?'

'Well – Sophist, I suppose, Socrates, is the name generally given to him.'

'Then it is as a Sophist that we will go to him and pay
him?'

'Yes.'

'And if you had to face the further question, what do you
yourself hope to become by your association with Pro- 312
tagoras . . .?'

He blushed at this – there was already a streak of daylight to betray him – and replied: 'If this is like the other
cases, I must say "to become a Sophist".'

'But wouldn't a man like you be ashamed' said I, 'to face
your fellow-countrymen as a Sophist?'

'If I am to speak my real mind, I certainly should.'

B   'Perhaps then this is not the kind of instruction you expect to get from Protagoras, but rather the kind you got from the schoolmasters who taught you letters and music and gymnastics. You didn't learn these for professional purposes, to become a practitioner, but in the way of liberal education, as a layman and a gentleman should.'

'That exactly describes' said he, 'the sort of instruction I expect from Protagoras.'

'Well then' I went on, 'do you understand what you are now going to do, or not?'

'In what respect?'

C   'I mean that you are going to entrust the care of your soul to a man who is, in your own words, a Sophist; though I should be surprised if you know just what a Sophist is. And yet if you don't know that, you don't know to whom you are entrusting your soul, nor whether he represents something good or bad.'

'I think I know' said he.

'Tell me then, what do you think a Sophist is?'

'I suppose, as the name implies, one who has knowledge of wise things.'

'One could say the same' said I, 'of painters and builders, that they are those who have knowledge of wise things.

D   But if we were asked what *sort* of wisdom painters understand, we should reply: wisdom concerned with the making of likenesses, and so on with the others. If then we were asked what sort of wise things the Sophist has knowledge of, what should we answer? Of what is he the master?'

'The only answer we could give is that he is master of the art of making clever speakers.'

'Well, our answer might be true, but would hardly be sufficient. It invites the further question, on what matter does the Sophist make one a clever speaker? For example,

B   the teacher of lyre-playing I suppose makes people clever at speaking on his own subject, namely lyre-playing, doesn't he?'

'Yes.'

'Well, on what subject does the Sophist make clever speakers?'

'Obviously on the subject of which he imparts knowledge.'

'Very probably. And what is this subject on which the Sophist is both an expert himself and can make his pupil expert?'

'I give up' he said. 'I can't tell you.'

'Well then' I continued, 'do you realize the sort of danger to which you are going to expose your soul? If it were a case of putting your body into the hands of someone and risking the treatment turning out beneficial or the reverse, you would ponder deeply whether to entrust it to him or not, and would spend many days over the question, calling on the counsel of your friends and relations; but when it comes to something which you value more highly than your body, namely your soul – something on whose beneficial or harmful treatment your whole welfare depends – you have not consulted either your father or your brother or any of us who are your friends on the question whether or not to entrust your soul to this stranger who has arrived among us. On the contrary, having heard the news in the evening, so you tell me, here you come at dawn, not to discuss or consult me on this question of whether or not to entrust yourself to Protagoras, but ready to spend both your own money and that of your friends as if you had already made up your mind that you must at all costs associate with this man – whom you say you do not know and have never spoken to, but call a Sophist, and then turn out not to know what a Sophist is though you intend to put yourself into his hands.'

When he heard this he said: 'It looks like it, Socrates, from what you say.'

'Can we say then, Hippocrates, that a Sophist is really a

313

B

C

merchant or peddler of the goods by which a soul is nourished? To me he appears to be something like that.'

'But what is it that nourishes a soul?'

'What it learns, presumably' I said. 'And we must see that the Sophist in commending his wares does not deceive us, like the wholesaler and the retailer who deal in food D for the body. These people do not know themselves which of the wares they offer is good or bad for the body, but in selling them praise all alike: and those who buy from them don't know either, unless one of them happens to be a trainer or a doctor. So too those who take the various subjects of knowledge from city to city, and offer them for sale retail to whoever wants them, commend everything that they have for sale; but it may be, my dear Hippocrates, that some of these men also are ignorant of the beneficial or E harmful effects on the soul of what they have for sale, and so too are those who buy from them, unless one of them happens to be a physician of the soul. If then you chance to be an expert in discerning which of them is good or bad, it is safe for you to buy knowledge from Protagoras or anyone else; but if not, take care you don't find yourself 314 gambling dangerously with all of you that is dearest to you. Indeed the risk you run in purchasing knowledge is much greater than that in buying provisions. When you buy food and drink, you can carry it away from the shop or warehouse in a receptacle, and before you receive it into your body by eating or drinking you can store it away at home and take the advice of an expert as to what you should eat and drink and what not, and how much you should consume and when; so there is not much risk in the actual B purchase. But knowledge cannot be taken away in a parcel. When you have paid for it you must receive it straight into the soul: you go away having learned it and are benefited or harmed accordingly. So I suggest we give this matter some thought, not only by ourselves, but also with those who are older than us; for we are still rather young to examine such a large problem. However, now let us carry out

our plan to go and hear the man, and when we have heard
him we can bring others into our consultations also, for
Protagoras is not here by himself. There is Hippias of Elis   c
and I think Prodicus of Ceos too, and many other wise
men.'

Having agreed on this we started out. When we found
ourselves in the doorway, we stood there and continued a
discussion which had arisen between us on the way. So
that we might not leave it unfinished, but have it out before
we went in, we were standing in the doorway talking until
we should reach agreement. I believe the porter, a eunuch,
overheard us, and it seems likely that the crowd of Sophists   D
had put him in a bad temper with visitors. At any rate when
we knocked at the door he opened it, saw us and said:
'Ha, Sophists! He's busy.' And thereupon he slammed the
door as hard as he could with both hands. We knocked
again, and he answered through the closed door: 'Didn't
you hear me say he's busy?'

'My good man' I said, 'we have not come to see Callias
and we are not Sophists. Cheer up. It is Protagoras we want   E
to see, so announce us.' So at last the fellow reluctantly
opened the door to us.

When we were inside, we came upon Protagoras walking
in the portico, and walking with him in a long line were, on
one side Callias son of Hipponicus, his step-brother Paralus
the son of Pericles, and Charmides son of Glaucon, and on   315
the other side Pericles's other son Xanthippus, Philippides
son of Philomelus, and Antimoerus of Mende, the most
eminent of Protagoras's pupils, who is studying profes-
sionally, to become a Sophist. Those who followed behind
listening to their conversation seemed to be for the most
part foreigners – Protagoras draws them from every city
that he passes through, charming them with his voice like
Orpheus, and they follow spellbound – but there were some   B
Athenians in the band as well. As I looked at the party I
was delighted to notice what special care they took never
to get in front or to be in Protagoras's way. When he and

those with him turned round, the listeners divided this way and that in perfect order, and executing a circular movement took their places each time in the rear. It was beautiful.

c 'After that I recognized', as Homer says, Hippias of Elis, sitting on a seat of honour in the opposite portico; and around him were seated on benches Eryximachus son of Acumenos and Phaedrus of Myrrhine and Andron son of Androtion, with some fellow-citizens of his and other foreigners. They appeared to be asking him questions on natural science, particularly astronomy, while he gave each his explanation *ex cathedra* and held forth on their problems.

D 'And there too spied I Tantalus' – for Prodicus of Ceos was also in town, and was occupying a room which Hipponicus used to use for storage, but now owing to the number of people staying in the house Callias had cleared it out and made it into a guest-room. Prodicus was still in bed, wrapped up in rugs and blankets, and plenty of them, as far as one could see; and beside him on the neighbouring couches sat Pausanias from Cerameis and with him someone who was still a young boy – a lad of fine character I

E think, and certainly very good-looking. I think I heard that his name is Agathon, and I shouldn't be surprised if Pausanias is particularly attached to him. Well there was this boy and the two Adimantuses – the son of Cepis and the son of Leucolophides – and a few others. But what they were talking about I couldn't discover from outside, although I was very keen to hear Prodicus, whom I regard

316 as a man of inspired genius. You see, he has such a deep voice that there was a kind of booming noise in the room which drowned the words. Just after we had come in, there entered close on our heels the handsome Alcibiades as you call him – and I quite agree – and Critias son of Callaischrus.

When we entered, then, we paused for a few moments to drink in the scene and then approached Protagoras, and I

said: 'Protagoras, this is Hippocrates, and it is you that B
we have come to see.'

'Do you wish to speak to me alone' he asked, 'or with
the others?'

'It is all the same to us' I replied. 'Hear what we have
come for and then decide for yourself.'

'And what have you come for?'

'Hippocrates here is one of our citizens, son of Apollodorus. He comes of a great and prosperous family, and
is considered the equal of any of his contemporaries in
natural gifts. I think he is anxious to make a name for him- C
self in the city, and he believes that the most likely way to
success is to become a pupil of yours. So now it is for you
to decide whether you think this calls for a conversation
between ourselves or with others.'

'I appreciate your forethought on my behalf, Socrates.
A man has to be careful when he visits powerful cities as a
foreigner, and induces their most promising young men to
forsake the company of others, relatives or acquaintances, D
older or younger, and consort with him on the grounds
that his conversation will improve them. Such conduct
arouses no small resentment and various forms of hostility
and intrigue. Personally I hold that the Sophist's art is an
ancient one, but that those who put their hand to it in
former times, fearing the odium which it brings, adopted a
disguise and worked under cover. Some used poetry as a
screen, for instance Homer and Hesiod and Simonides;
others religious rites and prophecy, like Orpheus and
Musaeus and their school; some even – so I have noticed –
physical training, like Iccus of Tarentum and in our own
day Herodicus of Selymbria, the former Megarian, as great E
a Sophist as any. Music was used as cover by your own
Agathocles, a great Sophist, and Pythoclides of Ceos and
many others. All of them, as I say, used these arts as a
screen to escape malice. I myself, however, am not of their
mind in this. I don't believe they accomplished their pur- 317
pose, for they did not pass unobserved by the men who

47

held the reins of power in their cities, though it is on their account that these disguises are adopted; the mass of people notice nothing, but simply echo what the leaders tell them. Now to run away and fail to escape, but be discovered B instead, turns the attempt into sheer folly, and cannot fail to arouse even greater hostility, for people think that the man who behaves like this is in addition to his other faults an unprincipled rogue. I therefore have always gone the opposite way to my predecessors. I admit to being a Sophist and an educator, and I consider this a better precaution than the other – admission rather than denial. I have devised other precautions as well, so that (if Heaven will C forgive the boast) I come to no harm through being a confessed Sophist, though I have been many years in the profession. Indeed I am getting on in life now – so far as age goes I might be the father of any one of you – so if there is anything you want of me, I should much prefer to say my say in front of the whole company.'

Thereupon, suspecting that he wanted to display his skill to Prodicus and Hippias and get some glory from the fact that we had come as his professed admirers, I remarked, D 'Then why should we not call Prodicus and Hippias, and the people who are with them, to listen to us?'

'By all means' said Protagoras.

'Would you like to make a regular circle' said Callias, 'so that you can talk sitting down?'

Everyone agreed that this was the thing to do, and at the prospect of listening to wise men we all eagerly took hold of the benches and couches with our own hands and arranged them beside Hippias, where the benches were. E Meanwhile Callias and Alcibiades got Prodicus out of bed and fetched him along with his companions.

When we were all seated, Protagoras began: 'Now that these gentlemen are present, Socrates, perhaps you will say something about the matter you mentioned to me just now on this young man's behalf.'

318 'I can only begin as I did before, by telling you of our

purpose in coming. Hippocrates has a feeling that he would like to become one of your followers. He says therefore that he would be glad to be told what effect it will have on him. That is all we have to say.'

Then Protagoras replied: 'Young man, if you come to me, your gain will be this: the very day you join me, you will go home a better man, and the same the next day. Each day you will make progress towards a better state.'

On hearing this I said: 'Protagoras, what you say is not **B** at all surprising, but very natural. Even you, for all your years and wisdom, would become better, if someone were to teach you something that you didn't happen to know. Please don't answer like this, but give us the kind of reply that Hippocrates would get if he suddenly changed his mind and took a fancy to study with that young man who has just lately come to live at Athens, Zeuxippus of Heraclea. Suppose he went to him, just as he has come to you, and heard him say the same thing, that each day he **C** spent with him he would get better and make progress, and asked him the further question: "What shall I get better at, and where shall I make progress?" Zeuxippus would say, "In painting." Or if he were with Orthagoras of Thebes, and having heard the same reply as he got from you, went on to ask in what respect he would get daily better by being with him, Orthagoras would say, "In playing the flute". Now give a similar answer to the lad and to me who am putting the question for him. Hippocrates, by becoming a pupil of **D** Protagoras, will, on the very day he joins him, go home a better man, and on each successive day will make similar progress – towards what, Protagoras, and better at what?'

Protagoras heard me out and said: 'You put your questions well, and I enjoy answering good questioners. When he comes to me, Hippocrates will not be put through the same things that another Sophist would inflict on him. The others treat their pupils badly: these young men, who have deliberately turned their backs on specialization, they **E** take and plunge into special studies again, teaching them arithmetic and astronomy and geometry and music' – here he glanced at Hippias – 'but from me he will learn only what he has come to learn. What is that subject? The proper care of his personal affairs, so that he may best manage his own household, and also of the State's affairs, 319 so as to become a real power in the city, both as speaker and man of action.'

'Do I follow you?' said I. 'I take you to be describing the art of politics, and promising to make men good citizens.'

'That' said he, 'is exactly what I profess to do.'

'Then it is a truly splendid accomplishment that you have mastered' said I, 'if indeed you have mastered it. I warn you that you will hear nothing from me but my real B mind. The fact is, I did not think this was something that could be taught, though when you say otherwise I cannot doubt your word. But it is up to me to say why I believe it cannot be taught nor furnished by one man to another. I hold that the Athenians, like the rest of the Hellenes, are sensible people. Now when we meet in the Assembly, then if the State is faced with some building project, I observe that the architects are sent for and consulted about the proposed structures, and when it is a matter of shipbuilding, the naval designers, and so on with everything which C the Assembly regards as a subject for learning and teaching. If anyone else tries to give advice, whom they do not consider an expert, however handsome or wealthy or nobly-born he may be, it makes no difference: the members reject him noisily and with contempt, until either he is shouted down and desists, or else he is dragged off or ejected by the police on the orders of the presiding magistrates. That is how they behave over subjects they consider technical. But when it is something to do with the D government of the country that is to be debated, the man who gets up to advise them may be a builder or equally well a blacksmith or a shoemaker, merchant or shipowner, rich or poor, of good family or none. No one brings it up against any of these, as against those I have just mentioned, that here is a man who without any technical qualifications, unable to point to anybody as his teacher, is yet trying to give advice. The reason must be that they do not think this is a subject that can be taught.

'And you must not suppose that this is true only of the community at large. Individually also the wisest and best B of our countrymen are unable to hand on to others the virtue which they possess. Pericles, for instance, the father of these two boys, gave them the very best education in everything that depends on teaching, but in his own special kind of wisdom he neither trains them himself nor hands 320 them over to any other instructor: they simply browse around on their own like sacred cattle, on the chance of picking up virtue automatically. To take a different example, Clinias, the younger brother of Alcibiades here, is a ward of that same Pericles, who for fear that Alcibiades would corrupt him, took him away and tried to give him a better upbringing by placing him in the household of Ariphron. Before six months were out, Ariphron gave him back: he could make nothing of him. I could mention plenty of B others too, excellent men themselves, who never made anyone else better, either their own relatives or others.

'With these facts in mind, Protagoras, I do not believe that virtue can be taught. But when I hear you speaking as I do, my scepticism is shaken and I suppose there is truth in what you say, for I regard you as a man of wide experience, deep learning, and original thought. If then you can demonstrate more plainly to us that virtue is something that can be taught, please don't hoard your wisdom but explain.'

'I shall not be a miser, Socrates' he replied. 'Now shall I, C as an old man speaking to his juniors, put my explanation in the form of a story, or give it as a reasoned argument?'

Many of the audience answered that he should relate it in whichever form he pleased. 'Then I think' he said, 'it will be pleasanter to tell you a story.

'Once upon a time, there existed gods but no mortal
D creatures. When the appointed time came for these also to
be born, the gods formed them within the earth out of a
mixture of earth and fire and the substances which are com-
pounded from earth and fire. And when they were ready to
bring them to the light, they charged Prometheus and
Epimetheus with the task of equipping them and allotting
suitable powers to each kind. Now Epimetheus begged
Prometheus to allow him to do the distribution himself –
E "and when I have done it" he said, "you can review it".
So he persuaded him and set to work. In his allotment he
gave to some creatures strength without speed, and equip-
ped the weaker kinds with speed. Some he armed with
weapons, while to the unarmed he gave some other faculty
and so contrived means for their preservation. To those
that he endowed with smallness, he granted winged flight
or a dwelling underground; to those which he increased
321 in stature, their size itself was a protection. Thus he made
his whole distribution on a principle of compensation,
being careful by these devices that no species should be
destroyed.

'When he had sufficiently provided means of escape from
mutual slaughter, he contrived their comfort against the
seasons sent from Zeus, clothing them with thick hair or
B hard skins sufficient to ward off the winter's cold, and
effective also against heat; and he planned that when they
went to bed, the same coverings should serve as proper and
natural bedclothes for each species. He shod them also,
some with hoofs, others with hard and bloodless skin.

'Next he appointed different sorts of food for them; to
some the grass of the earth, to others the fruit of trees, to
others roots. Some he allowed to gain their nourishment by
devouring other animals, and these he made less prolific,
while he bestowed fertility on their victims, and so pre-
served the species.

'Now Epimetheus was not a particularly clever person,
C and before he realized it he had used up all the available

powers on the brute beasts, and being left with the human race on his hands unprovided for, did not know what to do with them. While he was puzzling about this, Prometheus came to inspect the work, and found the other animals well off for everything, but man naked, unshod, unbedded, and unarmed: and already the appointed day had come, when man too was to emerge from within the earth into the daylight. Prometheus therefore, being at a loss to provide any means of salvation for man, stole from Hephaestus and Athena the gift of skill in the arts, together with fire – for without fire it was impossible for anyone to possess or use this skill – and bestowed it on man. In this way man acquired sufficient resources to keep himself alive, but had no political wisdom. This was in the keeping of Zeus, and Prometheus no longer had the right of entry to the citadel where Zeus dwelt; moreover the sentinels of Zeus were terrible; but into the dwelling shared by Athena and Hephaestus, in which they practised their art, he penetrated by stealth, and carrying off Hephaestus's art of working with fire, and the art of Athena as well, he gave them to man. Through this gift man had the means of life, but Prometheus, so the story says, thanks to Epimetheus, had later on to stand his trial for theft.

'Since, then, man had a share in the portion of the gods, in the first place because of his divine kinship he alone among living creatures believed in gods, and set to work to erect altars, and images of them. Secondly, by the art which they possessed, men soon discovered articulate speech and names, and invented houses and clothes and shoes and bedding and got food from the earth.

'Thus provided for, they lived at first in scattered groups; there were no cities. Consequently they were devoured by wild beasts, since they were in every respect the weaker, and their technical skill, though a sufficient aid to their nurture, did not extend to making war on the beasts, for they had not the art of politics, of which the art of war is a part. They sought therefore to save themselves by coming together and founding fortified cities, but when they gathered in communities they injured one another for want of political skill, and so scattered again and continued

c to be devoured. Zeus therefore, fearing the total destruction of our race, sent Hermes to impart to men the qualities of respect for others and a sense of justice, so as to bring order into our cities and create a bond of friendship and union. Hermes asked Zeus in what manner he was to bestow these gifts on men. ''Shall I distribute them as the arts were distributed – that is, on the principle that one trained doctor suffices for many laymen, and so with the other experts? Shall I distribute justice and respect for

D their fellows in this way, or to all alike?'' ''To all'' said Zeus. ''Let all have their share. There could never be cities if only a few shared in these virtues, as in the arts. Moreover, you must lay it down as my law that if any one is incapable of acquiring his share of these two virtues he shall be put to death as a plague to the city.''

'Thus it is, Socrates, and from this cause, that in a debate involving skill in building, or in any other craft, the Athenians, like other men, believe that few are capable of

E giving advice, and if someone outside those few volunteers to advise them, then as you say, they do not tolerate it – rightly so, in my submission. But when the subject of their counsel involves political wisdom, which must always

323 follow the path of justice and moderation, they listen to every man's opinion, for they think that everyone must share in this kind of virtue; otherwise the state could not exist. That, Socrates, is the reason for this.

'Here is another proof that I am not deceiving you in saying that all men do in fact believe that everyone shares a sense of justice and civic virtue. In specialized skills, as you say, if a man claims to be good at the flute or at some other art when he is not, people either laugh at him or are annoyed, and his family restrain him as if he were

B crazy. But when it comes to justice and civic virtue as a whole, even if someone is known to be wicked, yet if he publicly tells the truth about himself, his truthfulness, which in the other case was counted a virtue, is here considered madness. Everyone, it is said, ought to say he is good, whether he is or not, and whoever does not make such a claim is out of his mind; for a man cannot be without some share in justice, or he would not be human.

'So much then for the point that men rightly take all alike into their counsels concerning virtue of this sort, because they believe that all have a share in it. I shall next try to demonstrate to you that they do not regard it as innate or automatic, but as acquired by instruction and taking thought. No one is angered by the faults which are believed to be due to nature or chance, nor do people rebuke or teach or punish those who exhibit them, in the hope of curing them: they simply pity them. Who would be so foolish as to treat in that way the ugly or dwarfish or weak? Everyone knows that it is nature or chance which gives this kind of characteristics to a man, both the good and the bad. But it is otherwise with the good qualities which are thought to be acquired through care and practice and instruction. It is the absence of these, surely, and the presence of the corresponding vices, that call forth indignation and punishment and admonition. Among these faults are to be put injustice and irreligion and in general everything that is contrary to civic virtue. In this field indignation and admonition are universal, evidently because of a belief that such virtue can be acquired by taking thought or by instruction. Just consider the function of punishment, Socrates, in relation to the wrongdoer. That will be enough to show you that men believe it possible to impart goodness. In punishing wrongdoers, no one concentrates on the fact that a man has done wrong in the past, or punishes him on that account, unless taking blind vengeance like a beast. No, punishment is not inflicted by a rational man for the sake of the crime that has been committed (after all one cannot undo what is past), but for the sake of the future, to prevent either the same man or, by the spectacle of his punishment, someone else, from doing wrong again. But to hold such a view amounts to holding that virtue can be instilled by education; at all events the

C punishment is inflicted as a deterrent. This then is the view held by all who inflict it whether privately or publicly. And your fellow-countrymen the Athenians certainly do inflict punishment and correction on supposed wrong-doers, as do others also. This argument therefore shows that they too think it possible to impart and teach goodness.

D 'I think that I have now sufficiently demonstrated to you, first that your countrymen act reasonably in accepting the advice of smith and shoemaker on political matters, and secondly, that they do believe goodness to be something imparted by teaching. There remains the question which troubles you about good men, why it is that whereas they teach their sons the subjects that depend on instruction, and make them expert in these things, yet in their own brand of goodness they do not make them any better than others. On this, Socrates, I will offer you a plain argument rather than a parable as I did before. Think of it like this.

E Is there or is there not some one thing in which all citizens must share, if a state is to exist at all? In the answer to this question, if anywhere, lies the solution of your difficulty. If there is, and this one essential is not the art of building or forging or pottery but justice and moderation and holi-

325 ness of life, or to concentrate it into a single whole, manly virtue: if, I say, it is this in which all must share and which must enter into every man's actions whatever other occupation he chooses to learn and practise; if the one who lacks it, man, woman or child, must be instructed and corrected until by punishment he is reformed; and whoever does not

B respond to punishment and instruction must be expelled from the state or put to death as incurable: if all this is true, and in these circumstances our good men teach their sons other accomplishments but not this one thing, then think what extraordinary people good men must be! We have already shown that they believe it can be taught, both publicly and privately; but although virtue can be taught and cultivated, yet it seems they have their sons instructed in other arts, ignorance of which is no matter for capital punishment, but although if they are left ignorant of virtue and morally uncultivated they may be punished by death or exile – and not only death but alienation of property and in a word the ruin of their estates – are we to suppose that they neglect this side of their education? Don't they rather bestow every care and attention upon it? Of course they do, Socrates. They teach and admonish them from earliest childhood and throughout their lives. As soon as a child can understand what is said to him, nurse, mother, tutor, and the father himself vie with each other to make him as good as possible, instructing him through everything he does or says, pointing out: "this is right and that is wrong, this honourable and that disgraceful, this holy, that impious: do this, don't do that." If he is obedient, well and good. If not, they straighten him with threats and beatings, like a warped and twisted plank.

'Later on when they send the children to school, their instructions to the masters lay much more emphasis on good behaviour than on letters or music. The teachers take good care of this, and when boys have learned their letters and are ready to understand the written word as formerly the spoken, they set the works of good poets before them on their desks to read and make them learn them by heart, poems containing much admonition and many stories, eulogies, and panegyrics of the good men of old, so that the child may be inspired to imitate them and long to be like them.

'The music-masters by analogous methods instil self-control and deter the young from evil-doing; and when they have learned to play the lyre, they teach them the works of good poets of another sort, namely the lyrical, which they accompany on the lyre, familiarizing the minds of the children with the rhythms and melodies. By this means they become more civilized, more balanced, and better adjusted in themselves and so more capable in whatever they say or do; for rhythm and harmonious adjustment are essential to the whole of human life.

'Over and above this, they are sent to a trainer, so that a good mind may have a good body to serve it, and no one
c be forced by physical weakness to play the coward in war and other ordeals.

'All this is done by those best able to do it – that is, by the wealthy – and it is their sons who start their education at the earliest age and continue it the longest. When they have finished with teachers, the State compels them to learn
D the laws and use them as a pattern for their life, lest left to themselves they should drift aimlessly. You know how, when children are not yet good at writing, the writing-master traces outlines with the pencil before giving them the slate, and makes them follow the lines as a guide in their own writing; well, similarly the State sets up the laws, which are inventions of good lawgivers of ancient times, and compels the citizens to rule and be ruled in accordance with them. Whoever strays outside the lines, it punishes;
E and the name given to this punishment both among yourselves and in many other places is correction, intimating that the penalty corrects or guides.

'Seeing then that all this care is taken over virtue, both individually and by the State, are you surprised that virtue should be teachable, and puzzled to know whether it is? There is nothing to be surprised at. The wonder would be if it were not teachable.

'Why then, you ask, do many sons of good men turn out worthless? I will tell you this too. It is nothing surprising, if what I said earlier was true, that this faculty,
327 virtue, is something in which no one may be a layman if a state is to exist at all. If it is as I say – and most assuredly it is – consider the matter with the substitution of any art you like. Suppose a state could not exist unless we were all flute-players to the best of our ability, and everyone taught

everyone else that art both privately and publicly, and scolded the bad flute-player, and no one held back on this subject any more than anyone now begrudges information B on what is right and lawful or makes a secret of it as of certain other techniques. After all, it is to our advantage that our neighbour should be just and virtuous, and therefore everyone gladly talks about it to everyone else and instructs them in justice and the law. If then, as I say, it were so with flute-playing, and we all showed equal eagerness and willingness to teach one another, do you think, Socrates, that the sons of good players would become good players in their turn any more than the sons of bad ones? Not so, I think, but whoever had a son with the greatest c natural talent for the flute, his son would rise to fame, and a son without this talent would remain in obscurity. The son of a good performer would often be a poor one, and vice versa; but at any rate all would be good enough in comparison with someone who knew nothing of flute-playing at all.

'Now apply this analogy to our present condition. The man who in a civilized and humane society appears to you the most wicked must be thought just – a practitioner, as D one might say, of justice – if one has to judge him in comparison with men who have neither education nor courts of justice nor laws nor any constraint compelling them to be continually heedful of virtue – savages in fact like those whom the playwright Pherecrates brought on to the stage at last year's Lenaea. If you found yourself among such people – people like the man-haters of his chorus – you would be only too glad to meet a Eurybatus and a Phrynondas,* and would bitterly regret the very depravity of our E own society. But as it is you are spoilt, Socrates, in that all are teachers of virtue to the best of their ability, and so you think that no one is. In the same way if you asked who teaches the Greek language you would not find anyone; and again if you looked for a teacher of the sons of our artisans 328

* Notorious bad characters of the day.

in the craft which they have in fact learned from their father
to the best of their ability, and from his friends in the same
trade, there again I don't think it would be easy to point to
a master, though in the case of a complete tiro it would be
easy enough. Thus it is with virtue and everything else, so
that if we can find someone only a little better than the
others at advancing us on the road to virtue, we must be
B content. My claim is that I am one of these, rather better
than anyone else at helping a man to acquire a good and
noble character, worthy indeed of the fee which I charge
and even more, as my pupils themselves agree. On this
account I have adopted the following method of assessing
my payment. Anyone who comes to learn from me may
C either pay the fee I ask for or, if he prefers, go to a temple,
state on oath what he believes to be the worth of my
instruction, and deposit that amount.

'There, Socrates, you have both the parable and the argument by which I have sought to show that virtue is teachable and that the Athenians believe it to be so, and that at
the same time it is quite natural for the sons of good fathers
to turn out good for nothing, and vice versa. Why, even
the sons of Polyclitus, who are contemporaries of Paralus
and Xanthippus here, cannot hold a candle to their father,
nor can the sons of many other craftsmen. But it is too
D early to bring such a charge against these two: they are
young, and there is still promise in them.'

Here Protagoras brought to an end his long and magnificent display of eloquence. For a long time I gazed at him
spellbound, eager to catch any further word that he might
utter. When I saw that he had really finished, I collected
myself with an effort and said, turning to Hippocrates:
'Son of Apollodorus, how grateful I am to you for inducing
E me to come here. To have heard what Protagoras has just
said is something I value very highly. I used to think that it
was by no human diligence that good men acquired their
goodness, but now I am convinced. There is just one small
thing holding me back, which Protagoras I know will

easily explain, now that he has instructed us on so many points. It is true that if a man talked on these matters with any of our popular orators, he might possibly hear similar discourses from Pericles or some other proficient speaker; but if one asks any of them an additional question, like books they cannot either answer or ask a question on their own account. Ask them the smallest thing supplementary to what they have said, and like a gong which booms out when you strike it and goes on until you lay a hand on it, so our orators at a tiny question spin out a regular Marathon of speech. Protagoras on the other hand, though he is perfectly capable of long and splendid speeches as we have seen, has also the faculty of answering a question briefly, and when he asks one himself, of waiting and listening to the answer – a rare accomplishment.

'Now then Protagoras, there is just one small question left, your answer to which will give me all I want. You say that virtue is teachable, and there is no one I would believe sooner than you. But there is one thing which took me by surprise in your speech, and I should like you to fill this gap in my mind. You said that Zeus bestowed on men justice and respect for their fellows, and again at several points in your discourse justice and self-control and holiness and the rest were mentioned as if together they made up one thing, virtue. This is the point I want you to state for me with more precision: is virtue a single whole, and are justice and self-control and holiness parts of it, or are these latter all names for one and the same thing? That is what I still want to know.'

'Well, that is easy to answer' said he. 'Virtue is one, and the qualities you ask about are parts of it.'

'Do you mean' said I, 'as the parts of a face are parts – mouth, nose, eyes and ears – or like the parts of a piece of gold, which do not differ from one another or from the whole except in size?'

'In the first way, I should say; that is, they are in the relation of the parts of a face to the whole.'

329

B

C

D

E

61

'Then do men so share in these parts of virtue that some have one and some another, or must a man who possesses one of them possess them all?'

'By no means. Many men are brave but unjust, and others are just but not wise.'

'Are these also parts of virtue?' said I. 'Wisdom, I mean, and courage?'

330 'Most emphatically. Wisdom indeed is the greatest of the parts.'

'And each of them is different from the others?'

'Yes.'

'Has each also its own function? In a face, the eye is not like the ear nor has it the same function. Nor do the other parts resemble one another in function any more than in other respects. Is this how the parts of virtue differ, both in B themselves and in their function? It must be so, I suppose, if the parallel holds good.'

'Yes it is so, Socrates.'

'Then no other part of virtue resembles knowledge or justice or courage or temperance or holiness.'

He agreed.

'Now let us consider together what sort of thing each is. C First of all, is there such a thing as justice or not? I think there is.'

'So do I' he said.

'Well, if someone asked you and me: "Tell me, you two, this thing that you mentioned a moment ago – justice – is it itself just or unjust?" I myself should answer that it was just. Which way would you vote?'

'The same as you' he said.

'Then we would both answer that justice is of such a nature as to be just?'

He agreed.

D 'If he next asked: "You say that there is also such a thing as holiness?" we should agree I suppose?'

'Yes.'

'"Meaning that holiness too is a thing?" We should still assent?'

He agreed again.

'"Do you then say that this thing is of a nature to be holy or unholy?" Personally I should be annoyed at this, and say: "What a blasphemous question! Nothing else could well be holy if we won't allow holiness itself to be so." What about you? Wouldn't that be your answer?'

'Certainly' he said.

'Suppose now he went on to ask us: "But what did you say a few minutes ago? Didn't I hear you rightly? I thought you said that the parts of virtue are so related that one does not resemble the other"; for my part I should reply: "You have got most of it right, but your ears deceived you if you think I said that myself. It was Protagoras's answer to a question I put." Now if he asks you: "Is this true, Protagoras? Is it you who say that one part of virtue does not resemble another? Is this your statement?" – what would you answer?'

'I should have to admit it' he said.

'Then having agreed about this, what shall we say if he goes on to ask: "Then it is not the nature of holiness to be something just, nor of justice to be holy; it will be not-holy, and holiness will be not-just, that is unjust, and justice unholy?" What shall we answer? I should say on my own behalf that justice is holy and holiness just, and on your behalf, if you would allow me, I should make the same reply, that justice is either the same thing as holiness or very like it, and that justice unquestionably resembles holiness and holiness justice. Are you going to prevent me from making this answer, or do you agree with me?'

'I don't think it is quite so simple, Socrates. I can't really admit that justice is holy and holiness just; I think there is some difference there. However' he said, 'what does it matter? If you like, let us assume that justice is holy and holiness just.'

'Excuse me' I said. 'It isn't this "if you like" and "if

63

that's what you think" that I want us to examine, but you and me ourselves. What I mean is, I think the argument will be most fairly tested, if we take the "if" out of it.'

D 'Well of course' he replied, 'justice does have some resemblance to holiness. After all, everything resembles everything else up to a point. There is a sense in which white resembles black, and hard soft, and so on with all other things that present the most contrary appearances. Even the parts of the face, which we described earlier as

E having different functions and not being like each other, have a certain resemblance and are like each other in some way. So by your method you can prove, if you want to, that they too all resemble one another. But it is not right to call things similar because they have some one point of similarity, even when the resemblance is very slight, any more than to call things dissimilar that have some point of dissimilarity.'

At this I said in some surprise: 'And is this how you suppose justice to be related to holiness, that there is only a slight resemblance between them?'

'Not quite that, but not on the other hand in the way

332 that you seem to believe.'

'Well' said I, 'this line of argument doesn't seem to be agreeable to you, so let us drop it and look at something else that you said. You recognize the existence of folly?'

'Yes.'

'Is not wisdom altogether contrary to it?'

'Yes.'

'And when men act rightly and advantageously, do you regard them as acting temperately or not?'

'Temperately.'

'That is to say with temperance?'

B 'Of course.'

'And those who act wrongly act foolishly, and in doing so do not behave temperately?'

He agreed.

'Then foolish behaviour is the opposite of temperate?'

'Yes.'

'And foolish behaviour is the outcome of folly, and temperate of temperance?'

'Yes.'

'If something is done with strength, it is done strongly, and if with weakness weakly, if with speed quickly, and if with slowness slowly?'

'Yes.'

'What is done in the same manner is done by the same c agency, and if contrariwise, by the contrary?'

He agreed.

'Again' said I, 'you recognize the existence of the fair?'

He did.

'Has it any contrary except the foul?'

'No.'

'And the good too you recognize?'

'Yes.'

'Has it any contrary except the bad?'

'No.'

'And also high pitch in sound? And has it any other contrary but low?'

'No.'

'In short' said I, 'to everything that admits of a contrary there is one contrary and no more.'

He conceded the point.   D

'Now' said I, 'let us recapitulate our points of agreement. We agreed that each thing has one contrary and no more; that what is done in a contrary manner is done by a contrary agency; that a foolish action is contrary to a temperate one; and that a temperate action is performed with temperance and a foolish one with folly.'

He admitted all this.

'If then what is done in a contrary manner is done by a E contrary agency, and one action is performed with temperance and the other with folly – in a contrary manner and so by contrary agencies – then folly is the contrary of temperance.'

'It seems so.'

'Now you remember our earlier agreement that folly was the contrary of wisdom?'

'Yes.'

'And that one thing has one contrary?'

'Certainly.'

333 'Then which statement are we to give up? The dictum "one thing one contrary" or the statement that wisdom is a distinct thing from temperance, both being parts of virtue, and that in addition to each being distinct they are dissimilar both in themselves and in their functions, like the parts of a face? Which shall we renounce? The two statements are not very harmonious. They don't chime well together

B or fit in with each other. How could they, if one thing can have only one opposite, and yet though folly is only one thing, temperance as well as wisdom appears to be contrary to it? Isn't that the way of it, Protagoras?'

He agreed, though most reluctantly.

'Then must not temperance and wisdom be the same, just as earlier justice and holiness turned out to be much the same? Come now Protagoras, we must not falter, but complete our inquiry. Do you think that a man who commits an injustice acts temperately in committing it?'

C 'For my part I should be ashamed to agree to that' he replied. 'Of course many people do.'

'Well, shall I direct my argument against them or against you?'

'If you wish' he said, 'argue first against the proposition of the many.'

'It is all the same to me' said I, 'provided you make the replies, whether it is your own opinion or not. It is the argument itself that I wish to probe, though it may turn out that both I who question and you who answer are equally under scrutiny.'

D At first Protagoras began to make difficulties, alleging that it would be hard to conduct a discussion on these terms, but in the end he agreed to answer.

'Good' said I. 'Now let us start from the beginning. You believe that some people show temperance in doing wrong?'

'We will suppose so' he said.

'And to show temperance is to show good sense?'

'Yes.'

'Which means that in doing wrong they have planned well?'

'So be it.'

'If their wrong-doing is successful or unsuccessful?'

'If it is successful.'

'You agree that some things are good?'

'Yes.'

'And do you mean by good those things which are beneficial to men?'

'Not only those' he said. 'Even if they are not beneficial B to men, I still call them good.'

At this point I thought Protagoras was beginning to bristle, ready for a quarrel and preparing to do battle with his answers. Seeing this I became more cautious and proceeded gently with my questioning. 'Do you mean things 334 which are beneficial to no human being, or things that are not beneficial at all? Do you call them good also?'

'Of course not' he said. 'But I know plenty of things – foods, drinks, drugs, and many others – which are harmful to men, and others which are beneficial; and others again which, so far as men are concerned, are neither, but are harmful or beneficial to horses, and others only to cattle or dogs. Some have no effect on animals, but only on trees, and some again are good for the roots of trees but injurious to the young growths. Manure, for instance, is good for all B plants when applied to their roots, but utterly destructive if put on the shoots or young branches. Or take olive oil. It is very bad for plants, and most inimical to the hair of all animals except man, whereas men find it of service both to the hair and to the rest of the body. So diverse and multiform is goodness that even with us the same thing is good

C when applied externally but deadly when taken internally.
Thus all doctors forbid the sick to use oil in preparing their
food, except in the very smallest quantities, just enough to
counteract the disagreeable smell which food and sauces
may have for them.'

The audience vigorously applauded this speech. Then
said I: 'I'm a forgetful sort of man, Protagoras, and if
D someone speaks at length, I lose the thread of the argument. If I were a little deaf, you would recognize the necessity of raising your voice if you wanted to talk to me; so
now since you find me forgetful, cut down your answers
and make them shorter if I am to follow you.'

'What do you mean by "make my answers short"? Am
I to make them shorter than the subject demands?'

'Of course not.'

'As long as is necessary then?'

E 'Yes.'

'As long a reply as *I* think necessary, or *you*?'

'What they told me' I answered, 'is that you have the
gift both of speaking yourself, and of teaching others to
speak, just as you prefer; either at length, so that you never
335 run dry, or so shortly that no one could beat you for brevity. If then you are going to talk to me, please use the
second method and be brief.'

'Frankly, Socrates' said he, 'I have fought many a con-
test of words, and if I had done as you bid me, that is,
adopted the method chosen by my opponent, I should have
proved no better than anyone else, nor would the name of
Protagoras have been heard of in Greece.'

I saw that he was dissatisfied with his own performance
in the answers he had given, and would not of his own free
B will continue in the role of answerer, and it seemed to me
that it was not my business to remain any longer in the
discussions. 'Well' I said, 'I have no wish myself to insist
on continuing our conversation in a way that you don't
approve. I will talk with you another time, when you
are willing to converse so that I can follow. You for

68

your part, as others say and you say for yourself, can carry on a discussion both in long and short speeches, for you are a gifted man. I on the other hand cannot manage these long C speeches – I wish I could. It was for you, who can do both, to indulge me and so make our discussion possible. But since you would rather not, and I have something to do and could not stay while you spin out your long speeches, I will leave you. I really ought to be going. Otherwise I should probably be glad to hear them.'

With these words I got up to leave. As I did so Callias D caught my hand with his right hand, and with his left took hold of this old coat of mine and said: 'We shan't let you go, Socrates. Our talk won't be the same without you. Please stay with us. There is nothing that I would rather listen to than a conversation between you and Protagoras. You will be doing us all a kindness.'

I was already standing up to go, and answered: 'Son of Hipponicus, I have always admired your enthusiasm for wisdom. Believe me, I praise and love you for it now, and E would gladly do what you wish, if your request were within my power to fulfil. But it's as if you were to ask me to keep up with Crison, the runner from Himera, when he was in his prime, or to run a race against some three-miler or Marathon champion. I would say that to run with them 336 would please me even more than it would please you, but I can't do it: if you want to see me and Crison running together, you must ask him to lower his standards, for I can't run fast, but he can run slowly. So if you want to hear Protagoras and me, ask him to go on answering me as he did at first, briefly and keeping to the point of my questions. How can we have a discussion otherwise? Personally I B thought that companionable talk was one thing, and public speaking another.'

'But don't you see, Socrates?' he said. 'Protagoras is surely right in thinking that he is entitled to talk in the way that suits him, just as much as you are.'

Here Alcibiades broke in. 'No, no, Callias' he said.

69

'Socrates admits frankly that long speeches are beyond him
c and that Protagoras has the better of him there, but in discussion and the intelligent give and take of arguments I
doubt if he would give any man best. If Protagoras in his
turn admits that Socrates beats him in discussion, Socrates
will be satisfied. But if he maintains his claim, let him continue the discussion with question and answer, not meeting
every question with a long oration, eluding the arguments
and refusing to meet them properly, spinning it out until
d most of his hearers have forgotten what the question was
about – not that Socrates will be the one to forget it: I'll
guarantee that, in spite of his little joke about being forgetful. I hold then that what Socrates proposes is the more
reasonable, and I suppose it's right for each of us to say
what he thinks.'

After Alcibiades, so far as I remember, it was Critias
who spoke, addressing his remarks to Prodicus and
Hippias. 'Callias' he said, 'seems to me to be very much
e on the side of Protagoras, and Alcibiades is always out to
win when he takes up a cause. But it is not for us to be
partisans either of Socrates or of Protagoras. Let us implore
them both alike not to break up the discussion in mid
career.'

337 Hearing this, Prodicus began: 'You are quite right,
Critias. Those who are present at discussions of this kind
must divide their attention between the speakers impar-
tially, but not equally. The two things are not the same.
They must hear both alike, but not give equal weight to
each. More should be given to the wiser, and less to the
other. I add my plea, Protagoras and Socrates, that you
b should be reconciled. Let your conversation be a discussion
not a dispute. A discussion is carried on among friends
with goodwill, but a dispute is between rivals and enemies.
In this way our meeting will be best conducted. You, the
speakers, will be esteemed by us – esteemed, I say, not
praised, for esteem is a genuine feeling in the hearts of the
audience, whereas praise is often on the lips of men belying

their true conviction – and we who listen will experience   C
enjoyment rather than pleasure. Enjoyment can result from
learning and partaking in the intellectual activity of the
mind alone, but pleasure arises rather from eating or other
forms of physical indulgence.'

So said Prodicus, and a large number of those present
expressed agreement. After him the wise Hippias spoke up.
'Gentlemen' he said, 'I count you all my kinsmen and
family and fellow-citizens – by nature, not by convention.
By nature like is kin to like, but custom, the tyrant of man-   D
kind, does much violence to nature. For us then who
understand the nature of things, who are the intellectual
leaders of Greece and in virtue of that very fact are now
assembled in Athens, the centre and shrine of Greek wisdom, and in this the finest house of that city, it would be a
disgrace if we produced nothing worthy of our fame but   E
fell to bickering like the lowest of mankind.

'And so my request and my advice to you, Protagoras
and Socrates, is to be reconciled, allowing us to act as
mediators and bring you together in a compromise. Socrates should not insist on the strict forms of discussion,   338
carried on through the briefest of exchanges, if it is unwel-
come to Protagoras, but should give way and slacken the
reins of his discourse, so that it may wear for us a more
dignified and elegant air; and Protagoras should refrain
from shaking out every reef and running before the wind,
launching out on a sea of words till he is out of sight of
land. Let both take a middle course. Do this, take my
advice, and appoint an arbitrator, referee or president to   B
preserve a moderate length in the speeches of both of
you.'

This counsel won general consent and a round of applause. Callias refused to let me go and they told us to
choose an overseer. But I said that it would be unfitting to
choose an arbitrator over our words. If he were a man of
lesser attainments, it would be wrong to set him over
his betters, and if he were someone like ourselves it would

still not be proper; for in resembling us he would
c act like us, and his appointment would be superfluous.
'Well then, you will say, we will choose someone superior.'
But the fact is, in my opinion, that it would be impossible
for you to choose anyone wiser than Protagoras, and if
you choose some lesser man and pretend he is better, this
again would be to insult him, appointing someone over
him as if he were a nobody. For myself I am indifferent.

'I have another proposal to enable our discussion to
proceed as you wish it to. If Protagoras is unwilling to give
D replies, let him be the questioner and I will answer, and at
the same time try to show him how, in my submission, the
respondent should speak. When I have answered as many
questions as he likes to put, let him in return render similar
account to me. Then if he does not seem to wish to answer
a question as put, you and I will appeal to him jointly, as
you did to me, not to spoil the discussion. For this purpose
E we have no need of a single arbitrator; you will all keep
watch on us together.'

Everyone thought this was the right way to proceed.
Protagoras was most unwilling, but he had to agree to be
the questioner, and then when he had questioned me sufficiently, to submit himself to me in turn and make brief
replies.

He began his questions something like this. 'In my view,
Socrates, the most important part of a man's education is to
339 become an authority on poetry. This means being able to
criticize the good and bad points of a poem with understanding, to know how to distinguish them, and give one's
reasons when asked. My question to you therefore will
concern the subject of our present discussion, namely virtue, but transferred to the realm of poetry. That will be the
only difference. Simonides in one of his poems says to
Scopas son of Creon of Thessaly:

B   *Hard is it on the one hand to become*
    A good man truly, hands and feet and mind
    Four square, wrought without blame.

Do you know the piece, or should I recite it all to you?'

'There is no need' I said. 'I know it and have given it quite a lot of study.'

'Good. Now do you think it a beautiful and well written poem?'

'Yes, both beautiful and well written.'

'And do you think a poem beautifully written if the poet contradicts himself?'

'No.'

'Then look at it more closely.'   C

'But really I have given it enough thought.'

'Then you must know that as the poem proceeds he says:

> *Nor do I count as sure the oft-quoted word*
> *Of Pittacus, though wise indeed he was*
> *Who spoke it. To be noble, said the sage,*
> *Is hard.*

You understand that this is the same poet as wrote the previous lines?'

'Yes.'

'Then you think the two passages are consistent?'

'For my part I do' said I, though not without a fear that he might be right. 'Don't you?'

'How can a man be thought consistent when he says   D
both these things? First he lays it down himself that it is hard for a man to become truly good, then when he is a little further on in the poem he forgets. He finds fault with Pittacus, who said the same thing as he did himself, that it is hard to be noble, and refuses to accept it from him; but in censuring the man who said the same as he does, he obviously censures himself. Either his first or his second statement is wrong.'

This sally evoked praise and applause from many of the audience, and at first I was like a man who has been hit by a   E
good boxer: at his words and the applause things went dark and I felt giddy. Then I turned to Prodicus – and to tell you the truth, this was a move to gain time to con-

sider what the poet meant – and appealed to him by name.
'Prodicus' I said, 'Simonides is of course your fellow-
340 citizen; you ought to come to his aid. I think I will call on
you as the river Scamander in Homer called on the Simois
when hard pressed by Achilles, with the words:

Dear brother, let us both together stem the hero's might.

So I appeal to you lest our Simonides be sacked by Protagoras like another Troy, since truly to justify Simonides
calls for that art of yours whereby you discern the differ-
B ence between "wish" and "desire" and make all those
other elegant distinctions which we heard just now. So
see whether you agree with me. I don't believe Simonides
contradicts himself. Now let us have your opinion first.
Do you think "to become" and "to be" are the same, or
different?'

'Different, most certainly' said Prodicus.

'Well, at the beginning Simonides gave his own view,
that it is difficult to become a good man, didn't he?'

C 'True' said Prodicus.

'But as for Pittacus, he censures him not, as Protagoras
thinks, for saying the same thing, but something different.
According to Pittacus, the difficulty is not to *become* noble,
as Simonides said it was, but to *be*. As Prodicus says, Protagoras, to be and to become are not the same; and if to be
is not the same as to become, Simonides is not contradicting himself. I shouldn't be surprised if Prodicus and many
D others would agree with Hesiod that it is difficult to *become*
good – he says, you remember,

The gods have put sweat on the path to virtue;

but when

the summit's reached,
Hard though it was, thenceforth the task is light
To keep it.'

Prodicus commended my explanation, but Protagoras said:

'Your justification, Socrates, involves a greater error than the one it sets out to defend.'

'It seems then' said I, 'that I have done harm, and am a contemptible physician, whose cure inflames the disease.' B

'Well, it is so.'

'Explain' said I.

'The poet must be very stupid, if he says that it is such a light matter to hold on to virtue, when everyone agrees that there is nothing more difficult.'

To this I rejoined: 'It's a remarkably lucky thing that our friend Prodicus happens to be present at this discussion. I have a notion that his branch of wisdom is an old and god-given one, beginning perhaps with Simonides or going 341 even further back. Your learning covers many things but not, it appears, this. You are not acquainted with it as I have become through being a pupil of Prodicus. So now I don't think you understand that Simonides may not have taken this word "hard" as you do. It may be like the word "terrible" which Prodicus is always scolding me about, when in praising you or someone else I say "Protagoras is B a terribly clever person". He asks me if I'm not ashamed to call good things terrible. What is terrible, he says, is bad. No one speaks of "terrible wealth" or "terrible peace" or "terrible health", but rather of "a terrible disease", "a terrible war", "terrible poverty". Perhaps then the Ceans and Simonides understand "hard" as connoting something bad, or something else which you don't know. Let's ask Prodicus, for he is the right man to ask about the dialect of Simonides. C Prodicus, what does Simonides mean by "hard"?'

'Bad' he replied.

'Then that is why he blames Pittacus for saying "It is hard to be noble", just as if he had heard him saying that it was bad to be noble.'

'What else do you suppose Simonides means?' said Prodicus. 'He is reproaching Pittacus with not knowing how to distinguish meanings properly, being a Lesbian and brought up in a barbarous dialect.'

D   'Do you hear that, Protagoras?' said I. 'Have you anything to say to it?'

'It is not at all like that' said Protagoras. 'I know very well that by "hard" Simonides meant what the rest of us mean – not "bad", but what is not easy, only accomplished with much effort.'

'I believe myself that that is what Simonides meant' said I, 'and I am sure Prodicus knew it. He is joking, and wants to test your ability to stand up for your own opinion.

E Actually the very next words provide ample proof that Simonides did not equate "hard" with "bad". He goes on:

A god alone can have this privilege

and presumably he does not first say "it is bad to be noble" and then add that only a god could achieve it, and allot it as a privilege entirely divine. That would mean that Prodicus is calling Simonides quite unprincipled and no true Cean.

342 'However, I am ready to tell you my own opinion of Simonides's meaning in this song, if you wish to test my skill in poetry, as you call it; but if you prefer it I will listen to you.'

'Please speak if you will' said Protagoras when he heard this, and Prodicus, Hippias, and the others urged me strongly.

'Well then' said I, 'I will try to expound to you the view that I take. The most ancient and fertile homes of philosophy among the Greeks are Crete and Sparta, where are to

B be found more Sophists than anywhere on earth. But they conceal their wisdom like the Sophists Protagoras spoke of, and pretend to be fools, so that their superiority over the rest of Greece may not be known to lie in wisdom, but seem to consist in fighting and courage. Their idea is that if their real excellence became known, everyone would set to work to become wise. By this disguise they have taken in the pro-Spartans in other cities, who to emulate them go

about with bruised ears, bind their hands with thongs, take   **C**
to physical training and wear short cloaks, under the impression that these are the practices which have made the
Spartans a great power in Greece; whereas the Spartans,
when they want to resort freely to their wise men and are
tired of meeting them in secret, expel all resident aliens,
whether they be sympathizers with the Spartan way of life
or not, and converse with the Sophists unbeknown to any
foreigners. Conversely they don't allow any of their youths   **D**
to go abroad, for fear they should forget what they have
learned at home. No more do the Cretans. And in these
states there are not only men but also women who are
proud of their intellectual culture.

'Now this is how you may know that I am telling the
truth and that the Spartans are the best educated in philosophy and speaking: if you talk to the most ordinary
Spartan, you will find that for most of the time he shows   **B**
himself a quite unimpressive speaker. But then, at some
chance point in the conversation, like a brilliant marksman
he shoots in a telling phrase, brief and taut, showing up
whoever is talking to him to be as helpless as a child.

'Now there are some, both at the present day and in the
past, who have tumbled to this fact, namely that to be
Spartan implies a taste for intellectual rather than physical
exercise, for they realize that to frame such utterances is a   **343**
mark of the highest culture. Of these were Thales of Mile-
tus, Pittacus of Mitylene, Bias of Priene, our own Solon,
Cleobulus of Lindus and Myson of Chen, and the seventh
of their company, we are told, was a Spartan, Chilon. All
these were emulators, admirers and disciples of Spartan
culture, and their wisdom may be recognized as belonging
to the same category, consisting of pithy and memorable
dicta uttered by each. Moreover they met together and   **B**
dedicated the first-fruits of their wisdom to Apollo in his
temple at Delphi, inscribing those words which are on
everyone's lips: "Know thyself" and "Nothing too much".

'I mention these facts to make the point that, among the

ancients, this Laconic brevity was the characteristic expression of philosophy. In particular this saying of Pittacus, "Hard is it to be noble", got into circulation privately and earned the approval of the wise. It occurred therefore to Simonides, with his philosophic ambitions, that if he could floor this favourite maxim with a triumphant knockout, he would become the favourite of his own day. In my judgement he wrote the whole poem against the saying of Pittacus and on its account, in a deliberate effort to damage its fame.

'Now let us all examine it together, to see whether I am right. At the very beginning of the poem, it seems crazy, if he wished to say that it is hard to become a good man, that he should then insert "on the one hand". The insertion seems to make no sense, except on the supposition that Simonides is speaking polemically against the saying of Pittacus. Pittacus said "Hard is it to be noble", and Simonides replied, disputing the point, "No; to *become* a good man is hard truly" – not, by the way, "to become truly good": he does not refer the "truly" to that, as if some men were truly good and others good but not truly so. That would strike people as silly and unlike Simonides. We must transpose the word "truly" in the poem, thus as it were implying the saying of Pittacus before it, as if he spoke first and Simonides were answering his words. Thus: "O men, hard is it to be noble"; and Simonides replies, "That is not true, Pittacus; not to *be* but to *become* a good man, foursquare in hands and feet and mind, wrought without blame, that is hard truly".

'On this view we find that "on the one hand" comes in reasonably, and that "truly" finds its proper place at the end. Everything that follows bears out my opinion that this is the sense. Much could be said about each phrase in the poem to testify to the excellence of its composition – it is indeed an elegant and well thought out production – but to go through it in such detail would take too long. Nevertheless let us review its general character and intention, which is undoubtedly to constitute, throughout its length, a refutation of the saying of Pittacus.

'A little further on Simonides says, as if he were developing an argument, that although to become a good man is truly difficult, yet it is possible, for a while at least; "but having become good, to remain in this state and *be* a good man – which is what you were speaking of, Pittacus – is c impossible and super-human. This is the privilege of a god alone, whereas

> *he cannot but be bad, whom once*
> *Misfortune irredeemable casts down.*

Now who is cast down by irredeemable misfortune in the management of a ship? Clearly not the passenger, for he has *been* down all the time. You cannot knock down a man who is lying on the ground, you can only knock him down if he is standing, and put him on the ground. In the D same way irredeemable misfortune may cast down the resourceful, but not the man who is helpless all the time. The steersman may be reduced to helplessness by the onset of a great storm, the farmer by a bad season, and the doctor from some analogous misfortune; for the good may become bad, as another poet has testified in the line

> *The good are sometimes bad and sometimes noble;*

but the bad man cannot become bad, but *is* so of necessity. So it is that the resourceful and wise and good, when irre- E deemable disaster brings him to nought, cannot but be bad.

'You say, Pittacus, "Hard is it to be noble", whereas to *become* noble is hard, though possible, but to *be* so is impossible:

> *For when he fares well every man is good,*
> *But in ill-faring evil.*

Now what is faring well in letters, and what makes a man good at them? Clearly the learning of them. And what is 345 the faring well that makes a good doctor? Clearly it is

learning how to heal the sick. "But in ill-faring evil."
Who is it who becomes a bad doctor? Clearly a man who is
both a doctor and a good doctor: he might become a bad
doctor also. But we who are laymen in medicine could
never by faring ill become doctors or builders or any other
B kind of technician; and he who cannot by faring badly
become a doctor cannot, obviously, become a bad doctor.
Even so the good man may as easily be made bad, by lapse
of time or fatigue or illness or some other accident, seeing
that this is the only real ill-faring, to be deprived of knowledge. But the bad man cannot be made bad, for he is so all
the time. If he is to *become* bad, he must first become good.
C Thus this part of the poem also teaches the same lesson,
that to be a good man – continuing good – is not possible,
but a man may *become* good, and the same man bad; and
those are best for the longest time whom the gods love.

'All this, then, is aimed at Pittacus, and the next bit even
more plainly so, for he goes on:

> Then never shall I vainly cast away
> In hopeless search my little share of life,
> Seeking a thing impossible to be,
> A man all blameless, among those who reap
> The fruit of the broad earth. But should I find him
D > I'll send you word.

– See how violently, throughout the poem, he attacks the
saying of Pittacus –

> But all who do no baseness willingly
> I praise and love. The gods themselves strive not
> Against necessity.

This is all to the same purpose. Simonides was not so ignorant as to say that he praised all who did no evil voluntarily, as if there were any who did evil voluntarily. For
E myself I am fairly certain that no wise man believes anyone
sins willingly or willingly perpetrates any evil or base act.
They know very well that all evil or base action is involun-

tary. So here Simonides is not saying that he praises whoever does no evil willingly. The word "willingly" applies
to himself. His view was that a good man often forces him   346
self into love and praise, as when someone's mother or
father or native land is unsympathetic to him. The less
worthy, when they find themselves in such a position, seem
to accept it happily and expose the unworthiness of parents
or country with reproaches and denunciations, so that they
may neglect their duty towards them without thereby incurring the blame or reproaches of others. They even exaggerate their censure and add gratuitous hostility to that   B
which cannot be helped. Good men on the other hand conceal such faults and are constrained to praise, and if they feel
anger at some wrong done to them by parents or country,
they calm themselves and seek reconciliation, compelling
themselves to love and praise their own kin. No doubt
Simonides had in mind that he himself had often eulogized
a tyrant or someone of that stamp not of his own free will
but under compulsion.

'This then is addressed to Pittacus in particular, as if to   C
say: "My reason for blaming you, Pittacus, is not that I am
a fault-finder, for

> *to me that man suffices*
> *Who is not bad nor over-weak but sound*
> *In heart and knowing righteousness, the weal*
> *Of nations. I shall find no fault with him —*

I am not, he says, a censorious man —

> *For beyond number is the tribe of fools."*

So, he implies, if anyone takes pleasure in fault-finding, he
may have his fill in censuring them.

> *All is fair that is unmixed with foul.*

He does not say this in the sense in which he might have said
"all is white that is unmixed with black" — that would be   D
ridiculous on many counts — but meaning that for his part he

accepts without censure the middle state. "I do not seek" he has said

> *A man all blameless, among those who reap*
> *The fruit of the broad earth. But should I find him*
> *I'll send you word.*

If I wait for perfection I shall praise no one. For me it is enough if he reach the mean and do no evil, since

> *I praise and love all –*

note that he uses the Lesbian dialect here because he is addressing Pittacus –

> *I praise and love all willingly*

– this is where the pause is to be made in speaking it, at "willingly" –

> *who do no baseness,*

though there are those whom I praise and love against my will. If then you spoke with an even moderate degree of reasonableness and truth, Pittacus, I should never blame you. But as it is you have made an utterly false statement about something of the highest import, and it passes for true. For that I do blame you.

'That, gentlemen' I concluded, 'is my interpretation of the mind of Simonides in writing this poem.'

'This exposition of yours' said Hippias, 'seems to me highly meritorious. However, I also have an interesting thesis on the poem, which I will expound to you if you wish.'

'Yes, another time, Hippias' said Alcibiades. 'But at present Socrates and Protagoras must carry out their agreement. Let Socrates reply if Protagoras wants to ask further questions, or if he prefers to answer Socrates, then let Socrates do the questioning.'

Then said I: 'I leave it to Protagoras to do whichever pleases him. But if he is agreeable, I suggest we leave the subject of songs and poems, for I should be glad to reach a conclusion, Protagoras, in a joint investigation with you, on the matters about which I asked you at the beginning. Conversation about poetry reminds me too much of the wine-parties of second-rate and commonplace people. Such men, being too uneducated to entertain themselves as they drink by using their own voices and conversational re-sources, put up the price of female musicians, paying well for the hire of an extraneous voice – that of the pipe – and find their entertainment in its warblings. But where the drinkers are men of worth and culture, you will find no girls piping or dancing or harping. They are quite cap-able of enjoying their own company without such friv-olous nonsense, using their own voices in sober discussion and each taking his turn to speak or listen – even if the drinking is really heavy. In the same way gatherings like our own, if they consist of men such as most of us claim to be, call for no extraneous voices – not even of poets. No one can interrogate poets about what they say, and most often when they are introduced into the discussion some say the poet's meaning is one thing and some another, for the topic is one on which nobody can produce a conclusive argument. The best people avoid such discussions, and entertain each other from their own resources, testing one another's mettle in what they have to say themselves. These are the people, in my opinion, whom you and I should follow, setting the poets aside and conducting the conversation on the basis of our own ideas. It is the truth, and our own minds, that we should be testing. If you want to go on with your questions, I am ready to offer myself as an answerer; or if you prefer, be my respondent, to bring to its conclusion the discussion which we broke off in the middle.'

When I said this, and more to the same effect, Protagoras gave no clear indication of which he would do. Alcibiades then glanced at Callias and said: 'Do you still approve of what Protagoras is doing, refusing to say whether or not

he will be the answerer? I don't. Let him either continue
the discussion or tell us that he is unwilling, so that we may
know where we are with him, and Socrates can talk to
someone else, or any of the rest of us start a conversation.'

C   These words of Alcibiades, and requests from Callias
and almost all those present, made Protagoras feel ashamed,
or so I thought, and induced him to return reluctantly to
the discussion. He said therefore that he would answer and
told me to put my questions.

'Protagoras' I began, 'please don't think that I have any
other purpose in this discussion than to investigate questions which continually baffle me. I believe Homer hit a nail
on the head when he said

D   *If two go together, one perceives before the other.*

Somehow we all feel better fortified in this way for any
action or speech or thought. But to continue the quotation,
"If one alone perceive" – why he goes off at once looking
for someone to whom he can show his idea and with whom
he can confirm it, and will not rest till he finds him. That is
why I would rather talk to you than to anyone else, because
I think you are the most capable of elucidating the kind of
E   questions that a good man gives his mind to, and in particular the question of virtue. After all, whom else should I
look for? Not only are you, as you believe, an excellent
member of society yourself – there are some men very good
in themselves who cannot pass on their good qualities to
others – but you have also the ability to make others good,
and with such confidence that although some have made a
349   secret of their art you openly announce yourself to the
Greeks by the name of Sophist and set up as a teacher of
culture and virtue, the first to claim payment for this service. Naturally I must call on you for assistance in ponder-
ing these subjects and enlist you with me by asking you
questions. It could not be otherwise.

'I want then to go back to the beginning, to my first
questions to you on this subject. Some things I want you to

remind me of, and others I want to investigate with your B
help. The question, if I am not mistaken, was this. Wisdom,
temperance, courage, justice, and holiness are five terms.
Do they stand for a single reality, or has each term a particular entity underlying it, a reality with its own separate
function, each different from the other? Your answer was
that they are not names for the same thing, but that each of C
these terms applies to its own separate reality, and that all
these things are parts of virtue, not like the parts of a lump of
gold all homogeneous with each other and with the whole
of which they are parts, but like the parts of a face, resembling neither the whole nor each other and each having
a separate function. If you are still of the same mind, say so,
but if not, then declare yourself. I certainly shall not hold
you to your words if you now express yourself differently.
Very likely you spoke as you did to test me.' D

'No' he said. 'My view is that all these are parts of
virtue, and that four of them resemble each other fairly
closely, but courage is very different from all the rest. The
proof of what I say is that you can find many men who are
quite unjust, unholy, intemperate, and ignorant, yet outstandingly courageous.'

'Stop' said I. 'What you say merits investigation. Do E
you qualify the courageous as confident, or in any other
way?'

'As confident, yes, and keen to meet dangers from which
most men shrink in fear.'

'Then again, you consider virtue an honourable thing,
and it is on the assumption that it is honourable that you
offer to teach it?'

'Unless I am quite mad, it is the most honourable of all
things.'

'Part base and part honourable' I asked, 'or all honourable?'

'All honourable, as honourable as can be.'

'Now do you know which men plunge fearlessly into
tanks?'

'Yes, divers.'

'Is that because they know their job or for some other reason?'

'Because they know their job.'

'And what men feel confidence in a cavalry engagement? trained or untrained riders?'

'Trained.'

'And in fighting with the light shield – peltasts or non-peltasts?'

'Peltasts. And this holds good generally, if that is what you are after: those with the relevant knowledge have more confidence than those without it, and more when they have learned the job than they themselves had before.'

B   'But' said I, 'have you ever seen men with no understanding of any of these dangerous occupations, who yet plunge into them with confidence?'

'Indeed yes, with only too much confidence.'

'Then does not their confidence involve courage too?'

'No, for if so, courage would be something to be ashamed of. Such men are mad.'

'How then do you define the courageous? Did you not say they were the confident?'

C   'Yes, I still maintain it.'

'Well, those who are thus ignorantly confident show themselves not courageous but mad, and conversely, in the other case it is the wisest that are also most confident, and therefore most courageous? On this argument it is their knowledge that must be courage.'

'No, Socrates' he said. 'You have not remembered rightly what I said in my reply. When you asked me whether the courageous are confident, I agreed; but I was not asked whether the confident are also courageous – if

D   you had asked me that at the time, I should have said "not all of them" – and you have nowhere disproved my admission by showing that the courageous are not confident. Further, when you argue that those who have knowledge are more confident than they were before, and also than others who are ignorant, and thereupon conclude that courage and wisdom are the same thing, you might as well go on and conclude that physical strength is knowledge. First of all you would proceed to ask me whether the strong are powerful, and I should agree; next, whether those who B know how to wrestle are more powerful than those who do not, and more powerful after they have learned than before. Again I should agree, and it would then be open to you to say, adducing the same proofs, that on my own admission wisdom is physical strength. But here again I nowhere admit that the powerful are strong, only that the strong are powerful. Power and strength are not the same. Power can 351 result from knowledge, and also from madness or passion, whereas strength is a matter of natural constitution and bodily nurture. Similarly in our present discussion, I deny that confidence and courage are the same, and it follows that the courageous are confident but not all the confident are courageous. Confidence, like power, may be born of B skill, or equally of madness or passion, but courage is a matter of nature and the proper nurture of the soul.'

'Well' said I, 'you speak of some men living well, and others badly?'

He agreed.

'Do you think then that a man would be living well who passed his life in pain and vexation?'

'No.'

'But if he lived it out to the end with enjoyment, you would count him as having lived well?'

'Yes.'

'Then to live pleasurably is good, to live painfully bad?' C

'Yes, if one's pleasure is in what is honourable.'

'What's this, Protagoras? Surely you don't follow the common opinion that some pleasures are bad and some pains good? I mean to say, in so far as they are pleasant, are they not also good, leaving aside any consequence that they may entail? And in the same way pains, in so far as they are painful, are bad.'

'I'm not sure Socrates' he said, 'whether I ought to give
D an answer as unqualified as your question suggests, and
say that everything pleasant is good, and everything painful evil. But with a view not only to my present answer but
to the whole of the rest of my life, I believe it is safest to
reply that there are some pleasures which are not good, and
some pains which are not evil, others on the other hand
which are, and a third class which are neither evil nor
good.'

'Meaning by pleasures' said I, 'what partakes of pleasure or gives it?'

'Certainly.'

E 'My question then is, whether they are not, *qua* pleasant,
good. I am asking in fact whether pleasure itself is not a
good thing.'

'Let us' he replied, 'as you are so fond of saying yourself, investigate the question; then if the proposition we
are examining seems reasonable, and pleasant and good
appear identical, we shall agree on it. If not, that will be
the time to differ.'

'Good' said I. 'Will you lead the inquiry or should I?'

'It is for you to take the lead, since you introduced the
subject.'

352 'I wonder then' said I, 'if we can make it clear to ourselves like this. If a man were trying to judge, by external
appearance, of another's health or some particular physical
function, he might look at his face and hands and then
say: "Let me see your chest and back too, so that I may
make a more satisfactory examination". Something like
this is what I want for our present inquiry. Observing
that your attitude to the good and the pleasant is what you
say, I want to go on something like this: Now uncover another part of your mind, Protagoras. What is your attitude
B to knowledge? Do you share the common view about that
also? Most people think, in general terms, that it is nothing
strong, no leading or ruling element. They don't see it like
that. They hold that it is not the knowledge that a man

possesses which governs him, but something else – now passion, now pleasure, now pain, sometimes love, and frequently fear. They just think of knowledge as a slave, pushed around by all the other affections. Is this your view too, or would you rather say that knowledge is a fine thing quite capable of ruling a man, and that if he can distinguish good from evil, nothing will force him to act otherwise than as knowledge dictates, since wisdom is all the reinforcement he needs?'

'Not only is this my view' replied Protagoras, 'but I above all men should think it shame to speak of wisdom and knowledge as anything but the most powerful elements in human life.'

'Well and truly answered' said I. 'But I expect you know that most men don't believe us. They maintain that there are many who recognize the best but are unwilling to act on it. It may be open to them, but they do otherwise. Whenever I ask what can be the reason for this, they answer that those who act in this way are overcome by pleasure or pain or some other of the things I mentioned just now.'

'Well, Socrates, it's by no means uncommon for people to say what is not correct.'

'Then come with me and try to convince them, and show what really happens when they speak of being overcome by pleasure and therefore, though recognizing what is best, failing to do it. If we simply declare: "You are wrong, and what you say is false", they will ask us: "If it is not being overcome by pleasure, what can it be? What do you two say it is? Tell us."'

'But why must we look into the opinions of the common man, who says whatever comes into his head?'

'I believe' I replied, 'that it will help us to find out how courage is related to the other parts of virtue. So if you are content to keep to our decision, that I should lead the way in whatever direction I think we shall best see the light, then follow me. Otherwise, if you wish, I shall give it up.'

'No, you are right' he said. 'Carry on as you have begun.'

c 'To return then: If they should ask us: "What is your name for what we called being worsted by pleasure?" I should reply: "Listen. Protagoras and I will try to explain it to you. We take it that you say this happens to you when, for example, you are overcome by the desire of food or drink or sex – which are pleasant things – and though you recognize them as evil, nevertheless indulge in them." They would agree. Then we should ask them: "In what

D respect do you call them evil? Is it because for the moment each of them provides its pleasure and is pleasant, or because they lay up for the future disease or poverty or such-like? If they led to none of these things, but produced pure enjoyment, would they nevertheless be evils – no matter why or how they give enjoyment?" Can we expect any other answer than this, that they are not evil on account

E of the actual momentary pleasure which they produce, but on account of their consequences, disease and the rest?'

'I believe that would be their answer' said Protagoras.

'"Well, to cause disease and poverty is to cause pain." They would agree, I think?'

354 He nodded.

'"So the only reason why these pleasures seem to you to be evil is, we suggest, that they result in pains and deprive us of future pleasures." Would they agree?'

We both thought they would.

'Now suppose we asked them the converse question: "You say also that pains may be good. You mean, I take it, such things as physical training, military campaigns, doc-tors' treatment involving cautery or the knife or drugs or starvation diet? These, you say, are good but painful?" Would they agree?'

'They would.'

B '"Do you then call them good in virtue of the fact that at the time they cause extreme pain and agony, or because in the future there result from them health, bodily well-being,

the safety of one's country, dominion over others, wealth?"
The latter, I think they would agree.'

Protagoras thought so too.

'"And are they good for any other reason than that their
outcome is pleasure and the cessation or prevention of
pain? Can you say that you have any other end in mind, c
when you call them good, than pleasures or pains?" I
think they would say no.'

'I too' said he.

'"So you pursue pleasure as being good, and shun pain
as evil?"'

He agreed.

'"Then your idea of evil is pain, and of good is pleasure.
Even enjoying yourself you call evil whenever it leads to
the loss of a pleasure greater than its own, or lays up pains
that outweigh its pleasures. If it is in any other sense, or D
with anything else in mind, that you call enjoyment evil,
no doubt you could tell us what it is: but you cannot."'

'I agree that they cannot' said Protagoras.

'"Isn't it the same when we turn back to pain? To suffer
pain you call good when it either rids us of greater pains
than its own or leads to pleasures that outweigh them. If
you have anything else in mind when you call the actual E
suffering of pain a good thing, you could tell us what it is;
but you cannot."'

'True' said Protagoras.

'"Now my good people"' I went on '"If you ask me:
What is the point of all this rigmarole? I beg your indulgence. It isn't easy to explain the real meaning of what you
call being overcome by pleasure, and any explanation is
bound up with this point. You may still change your
minds, if you can say that the good is anything other than 355
pleasure, or evil other than pain. Is it sufficient for you to
live life through with pleasure and without pain? If so, and
you can mention no good or evil which cannot in the last
resort be reduced to these, then listen to my next point.

'"This position makes your argument ridiculous. You

91

say that a man often recognizes evil actions as evil, yet
commits them, under no compulsion, because he is led on
B and distracted by pleasure; and on the other hand that,
recognizing the good, he refrains from following it because
he is overcome by the pleasures of the moment. The ab-
surdity of this will become evident if we stop using all
these names together – pleasant, painful, good and evil
– and since they have turned out to be only two, call them
by only two names – first of all good and evil, and only at a
different stage pleasure and pain. Having agreed on this,
C suppose we now say that a man does evil though he recognizes it as evil. Why? Because he is overcome. By what?
We can no longer say 'by pleasure', because it has changed
its name to good. 'Overcome' we say. 'By what?' we are
asked. 'By the good', I suppose we shall say. I fear that if
our questioner is ill-mannered, he will laugh and retort:
D 'What ridiculous nonsense, for a man to do evil, knowing
it is evil and that he ought not to do it, because he is overcome by good. Am I to suppose that the good in you is or
is not a match for the evil?' Clearly we shall reply that the
good is not a match; otherwise the man whom we speak
of as being overcome by pleasure would not have done
wrong. 'And in what way' he may say, 'does good fail to
be a match for evil, or evil for good? Is it not by being
greater or smaller, more or less than the other?' We shall
E have to agree. 'Then by being overcome you must mean
taking greater evil in exchange for lesser good.'

'"Having noted this result, suppose we reinstate the
names pleasant and painful for the same phenomena, thus: A
man does – *evil* we said before, but now we shall say *painful*
actions, knowing them to be painful, because overcome by
pleasures – pleasures, obviously, which were not a match
for the pains. And what meaning can we attach to the
356 phrase *not a match for*, when used of pleasure in relation to
pain, except the excess or deficiency of one as compared
with the other? It depends on whether one is greater or
smaller, more or less intense than the other. If anyone

objects that there is a great difference between present
pleasure and pleasure or pain in the future, I shall reply
that the difference cannot be one of anything else but pleasure and pain. So, like an expert in weighing, put the pleas-   B
ures together and the pains together, set both the near and
distant in the balance, and say which is the greater quantity.
In weighing pleasures against pleasures, one must always
choose the greater and the more; in weighing pains against
pains, the smaller and the less: whereas in weighing pleasures against pains, if the pleasures exceed the pains, whether
the distant, the near or vice versa, one must take the course
which brings those pleasures; but if the pains outweigh the   C
pleasures, avoid it. Is this not so, good people?" I should
say, and I am sure they could not deny it.'

Protagoras agreed.

'"That being so then, answer me this" I shall go on.
"The same magnitudes seem greater to the eye from near at
hand than they do from a distance. This is true of thickness
and also of number, and sounds of equal loudness seem
greater near at hand than at a distance. If now our hap-   D
piness consisted in doing, I mean in choosing, greater
lengths and avoiding smaller, where would lie salvation?
In the art of measurement or in the impression made by
appearances? Haven't we seen that the appearance leads us
astray and throws us into confusion so that in our actions
and our choices between great and small we are constantly
accepting and rejecting the same things; whereas the metric
art would have cancelled the effect of the impression, and   E
by revealing the true state of affairs would have caused the
soul to live in peace and quiet and abide in the truth, thus
saving our life?" Faced with these considerations, would
people agree that our salvation would lie in the art of
measurement?'

He agreed that they would.

'Again, what if our welfare lay in the choice of odd and
even numbers, in knowing when the greater number must
rightly be chosen and when the less, whether each sort in

357 relation to itself or one in relation to the other, and whether they were near or distant? What would assure us a good life then? Surely knowledge, and specifically a science of measurement, since the required skill lies in the estimation of excess and defect; or to be more precise, arithmetic, since it deals with odd and even numbers. Would people agree with us?'

Protagoras thought they would.

B 'Well then (I shall say), since our salvation in life has turned out to lie in the correct choice of pleasure and pain – more or less, greater or smaller, nearer or more distant – is it not in the first place a question of measurement, consisting as it does in a consideration of relative excess, defect or equality?'

'It must be.'

'And if so, it must be a special skill or branch of knowledge.'

'Yes, they will agree.'

'"What skill, or what branch of knowledge it is, we shall leave till later; the fact itself is enough for the purposes of C the explanation which you have asked for from Protagoras and me. To remind you of your question, it arose because we two agreed that there was nothing more powerful than knowledge, but that wherever it is found it always has the mastery over pleasure and everything else. You on the other hand, who maintain that pleasure often masters even the man who knows, asked us to say what this experience D really is, if it is not being mastered by pleasure. If we had answered you straight off that it is ignorance, you would have laughed at us, but if you laugh at us now, you will be laughing at yourselves as well; for you have agreed that when people make a wrong choice of pleasures and pains – that is, of good and evil – the cause of their mistake is lack of knowledge. We can go further, and call it, as you E have already agreed, a science of measurement; and you know yourselves that a wrong action which is done without knowledge is done in ignorance. So that is what 'being mastered by pleasure' really is – ignorance, and most serious ignorance, the fault which Protagoras, Prodicus, and Hippias profess to cure. You on the other hand, because you believe it to be something else, neither go nor send your children to these Sophists, who are the experts in such matters. Holding that it is nothing that can be taught, you are careful with your money and withhold it from them – a bad policy both for yourselves and for the community." 358

'That then is the answer we should make to the ordinary run of people; and I ask you – Hippias and Prodicus as well as Protagoras, for I want you to share our discussion – whether you think what I say is true.'

They all agreed most emphatically that it was true.

'You agree then' said I, 'that the pleasant is good and the painful bad. I ask exemption from Prodicus's precise verbal distinctions. Whether you call it pleasant, agreeable or enjoyable, my dear Prodicus, or whatever name you like to apply to it, please answer in the sense of my request.' B

Prodicus laughed and assented, and so did the others.

'Well, here is another point' I continued. 'All actions aimed at this end, namely a pleasant and painless life, must be fine actions, that is, good and beneficial.'

They agreed.

'Then if the pleasant is the good, no one who either knows or believes that there is another possible course of action, better than the one he is following, will ever continue on his present course when he might choose the better. To "act beneath yourself" is the result of pure ignorance, to "be your own master" is wisdom.' C

All agreed.

'And may we define ignorance as having a false opinion and being mistaken on matters of great moment?'

They approved this too.

'Then it must follow that no one willingly goes to meet evil or what he thinks to be evil. To make for what one D believes to be evil, instead of making for the good, is not, it seems, in human nature; and when faced with the choice of two evils no one will choose the greater when he might choose the less.'

General agreement again.

'Now you recognize the emotion of fear or terror. I wonder if you conceive it as I do? (I say this to you, Prodicus.) Whether you call it fear or terror, I define it as expectation of evil.'

B   Protagoras and Hippias thought this covered both fear and terror, but Prodicus said it applied to fear but not to terror.

'Well Prodicus' said I, 'it makes no difference. This is the point. If what I have said is true, will anyone be willing to go to meet what he fears, when it is open to him to go in the opposite direction? Do not our agreed conclusions make this impossible? It is admitted that what he fears he regards as evil, and that no one willingly meets or accepts what he thinks evil.'

359   They all assented.

'On this agreed basis' I went on, 'let Protagoras make his defence and show us how his original answer can be right. I don't mean what he said at the very beginning, when he maintained that there were five parts of virtue none of which resembled any other, and that each had its separate function, but what he said later, that four of them

B   are fairly similar, but one, namely courage, is quite different from the rest. This, he said, the following evidence would show me: "You will find, Socrates, men who are utterly impious, unjust, licentious, and ignorant, yet very brave, which will show you that courage is quite different from the other parts of virtue." I was much surprised by this answer at the time, and now that we have had this discussion it surprises me even more. Anyway, I asked him if he described the brave as confident, and he replied "Yes, and

C   eager". Do you remember saying this, Protagoras?'

He admitted it.

'Tell me then' said I, 'in what direction are the brave eager to go? Towards the same things as cowards?'

'No.'

'Towards something else then?'

'Yes.'

'Is it that cowards go to meet what inspires confidence, and brave men to what is terrible?'

'So men say, Socrates.'

'I know they do, but that was not my question. What do **D** *you* say brave men go eagerly to meet? Is it what is terrible, knowing it to be terrible?'

'Your own argument has shown that to be impossible.'

'True again, so that if my argument was sound, no one goes to meet what he believes to be terrible, since not being one's own master was shown to be due to ignorance.'

He admitted this.

'But as for what inspires confidence, everyone makes for that, cowards and brave men alike, and thus cowards and brave men make for the same things.'

'Whatever you say' he replied, 'what the coward makes **E** for is precisely the opposite of what the brave man makes for. For instance, the brave are willing to enter battle, the others are not.'

'Is this willingness an honourable thing, or disgraceful?'

'Honourable' said he.

'Then if honourable, we agreed earlier that it is good, for we agreed that all honourable actions are good.'

'That is true, and I still think so.'

'Quite rightly too' said I. 'But which class did you say **360** were unwilling to enter battle although that is a fine and good thing to do?'

'The cowards' he replied.

'Well, if it is honourable and good, it is also pleasant.'

'We certainly agreed that.'

'Then do the cowards act with knowledge when they refuse to approach what is the more honourable and better and pleasanter thing?'

'If we say so' he replied, 'we shall confound our former conclusions.'

'Now take the brave man. He makes for what is more honourable, better and pleasanter?'

B 'I cannot deny it.'

'And in general when the brave feel fear, there is no disgrace in their fears, nor in their confidence when they are confident?'

'True.'

'So both are honourable, and if honourable then good?'

'Yes.'

'Cowards on the other hand, and likewise the rash and the mad, feel fears or confidence which are discreditable, and can they exhibit discreditable fear or confidence from any other cause than ignorance?'

'No.'

C 'Well then, is it cowardice or courage that makes a man a coward?'

'Cowardice.'

'Yet we have seen that it is ignorance of what is to be feared that makes them cowards; and if this ignorance makes them cowards, and you agree that what makes them cowards is cowardice, ignorance of what is and is not to be feared must be cowardice.'

He nodded.

D 'Well, courage is the opposite of cowardice' – he agreed –'and knowledge of what is and is not to be feared is the opposite of ignorance of these things' – he nodded again – 'which is cowardice' – here he assented with great reluctance – 'therefore knowledge of what is and is not to be feared is courage.'

At this point he could no longer bring himself to assent, but was silent; so I said: 'What, Protagoras, won't you say either yes or no to my questions?'

'Finish it yourself' said he.

E 'Just one more question first' I replied. 'Do you still

believe, as you did at first, that men can be utterly ignorant yet very brave?'

'You seem to be bent on having your own way, Socrates, and getting me to give the answers: so to humour you, I will say that on our agreed assumptions it seems to be impossible.'

'I assure you' said I, 'that in asking all these questions I have nothing else in view but my desire to learn the truth about virtue and what it is in itself. I know that if we could 361 be clear about that, it would throw the fullest light on the question over which you and I have spun such a coil of argument, I maintaining that virtue was not teachable and you that it was. It seems to me that the present outcome of our talk is pointing at us, like a human adversary, the finger of accusation and scorn. If it had a voice it would say: "What an absurd pair you are, Socrates and Protagoras. One of you, having said at the beginning that virtue is not teachable, now is bent upon contradicting himself by try- B ing to demonstrate that everything is knowledge – justice, temperance, and courage alike – which is the best way to prove that virtue *is* teachable. If virtue were something other than knowledge, as Protagoras tried to prove, obviously it could not be taught. But if it turns out to be, as a single whole, knowledge (which is what you are urging, Socrates), then it will be most surprising if it cannot be taught. Protagoras on the other hand, who at the beginning supposed it to be teachable, now on the contrary seems to be bent on showing that it is almost anything rather than C knowledge; and this would make it least likely to be teach-able."

'For my part, Protagoras, when I see the subject in such utter confusion I feel the liveliest desire to clear it up. I should like to follow up our present talk with a determined attack on virtue itself and its essential nature. Then we could return to the question whether or not it can be taught, thus guarding against the possibility that your Epimetheus might trip us up and cheat us in our inquiry, just as accord- D ing to the story he overlooked us in the distribution. I liked Prometheus in the myth better than Epimetheus, so I follow his lead and spend my time on all these matters as a means of taking forethought for my whole life. If you should be willing, then as I said at the beginning, you are the one with whom I would most gladly share the inquiry.'

'I congratulate you on your keenness, Socrates,' responded Protagoras, 'and your skill in exposition. I hope

B I am not too bad a character, and I am the last man to be jealous. I have told a great many people that I never met anyone I admire nearly as much as you, certainly not among your contemporaries; and I say now that I should not be surprised if you became one of our leading philosophers. Well, we will talk of these matters at some future meeting, whenever you like; but now it is time to turn to other things.'

362 'So be it' said I, 'if that is your wish. Indeed I ought long ago to have kept the appointment I mentioned. I only stayed as a concession to the blandishments of Callias.'

That was the end of the conversation, and we went away.

THE MENO

DRAMATIC DATE

THE introduction of Anytus and Socrates's reference to his
important position in the state show that the conversation
is supposed to take place after the restoration of the democracy in 403. On the other hand, Meno joined the expedition of Cyrus (the *Anabasis* of Xenophon) in March 401, and
never returned from it. We may therefore place the conversation in 402, some thirty years later than the meeting
described in the *Protagoras*. Socrates is already in his late
sixties, and his trial and condemnation are drawing near.

SPEAKERS IN THE DIALOGUE

Socrates.

Meno. The character of Meno as a wealthy, handsome and
imperious young aristocrat, visiting Athens from his
native Thessaly, is well brought out in the dialogue itself. He is a friend of Aristippus, the head of the Aleuadae who were the ruling family in Thessaly, and his own
family are *xenoi* (herditary guest-friends) of the Persian
king, a tie which must have dated from the time of
Xerxes, who made use of Thessalian hospitality on his
expedition against Greece. He knows the famous Sophist
and rhetorician Gorgias, who had stayed at Larissa in
Thessaly as well as meeting him in Athens. From Gorgias
he has acquired a taste for the intellectual questions of the
day, as seen through the eyes of the Sophists, whose trick
question about the impossibility of knowledge comes
readily to his lips.

Xenophon tells of his career as one of the Greek mer-
cenaries of Cyprus and gives him a bad character, describing him as greedy, power-loving, and incapable of

understanding the meaning of friendship. This account is probably prejudiced by Xenophon's admiration for the Greek leader Clearchus, a grim and hardly likeable character, whose rival and personal enemy Meno was. There were rumours that Meno entered into treacherous relations with the Great King, but he appears to have been finally put to death by him after the failure of the expedition, though possibly later than his fellow-prisoners.

Anytus. A prominent Athenian democrat in the last stages of the Peloponnesian War, exiled by the Thirty in 404, and in the next year an ally of Thrasybulus in the restoration of the democracy. One of the accusers of Socrates at his trial in 399, a fact of which Plato makes effective dramatic use both in the episode in which he takes part and in the final words of Socrates to Meno.

A Slave of Meno.

MENO asks Socrates how 'virtue' (*arete*) is acquired, whether by instruction or in some other way. Socrates replies that he cannot answer, because he does not yet know what it is. (We notice that this opening remark of Socrates is that with which he ended his discussion with Protagoras.) Meno is surprised; *he* can tell him what it is, and proceeds to do so by saying that there are different kinds for different people and enumerating them. Socrates points out that since all these are called by the same name they presumably have something in common, and suggests that it is this 'something in common' which they must look for if they are going to say what virtue is as such. Meno is eventually brought to agree, and proposes a definition ('the capacity to govern men') which Socrates demolishes. He then demonstrates by means of the examples *shape* and *colour* the kind of general definition that he wants. Meno tries again and is again put to confusion. His new definition, that virtue is 'the desire of fine – or good – things and the power to acquire them', will not do because (a) everyone in fact desires what is good, (b) the power of obtaining good things is only virtuous if we add 'justly but not unjustly'. Since justice has already been agreed to be a part of virtue, we are going round in a circle.

At this point Meno utters his despairing protest that the whole effect of Socrates's conversation is to induce numbness of the brain in his interlocutor and deprive him of the power of coherent thought. Socrates excuses himself by saying that at least he does not do this intentionally, from the position of one who knows, deliberately confusing a fellow-being who is seeking knowledge. So in this matter of virtue, he does not know what it is, and all that he has done is to show that Meno too, although he wrongly thought he knew, is in the same position. Now that both of them have admitted their ignorance, they can better co-operate in a joint effort to find the answer to their question.

This prompts Meno, by a natural turn in the conversation, to propound a sophistic dilemma about knowledge. One can never find out anything new: either one knows it already, in which case there is no need to find it out, or else one does not, and in that case there is no means of recognizing it when found. It is as a way out of this dilemma that Socrates propounds the theory of knowledge as recollection. This is bound up, he says, with the doctrine of certain religious teachers that the human soul is immortal. It does not perish at death, but migrates elsewhere, and in due course is born again in a new body. In the course of its wanderings, both here and in another world, it has learned all there is to know, the more easily because 'all nature is akin'. In this life therefore it is possible, starting from something which we consciously know, to be reminded of all the rest of the knowledge which is stored latent in our minds, and this is the real nature of the process which is commonly called learning. Meno asks for a demonstration that this is so, and there follows the experiment with the young slave, who though ignorant of mathematics is made by Socrates to solve a mathematical problem assisted only by questioning. Socrates claims that in this experiment he has not told the slave anything, but only, by his questions, elicited knowledge which must have been in the boy's mind, although he had hitherto been unaware that he possessed it.

At the end of this episode, Socrates disclaims certainty for every detail of the doctrine, but reiterates his conviction that it is not a hopeless task to seek diligently for knowledge which we do not believe ourselves to possess, and far better than weakly giving up the quest. He asks Meno therefore to resume their inquiry into the real nature of virtue.

Meno agrees, but says that he would much rather discuss his original question: can virtue be taught or not? Socrates protests once more that this is to invert the logical order – one ought not to ask whether a thing has a particular accidental quality before determining its essential nature – but consents on condition that Meno will allow him to proceed by means of a hypothesis about the nature of virtue. We say to ourselves, 'If virtue is teachable it must be x', and ask ourselves what value of x will satisfy the condition. The obvious answer is that it must be knowledge. Meno's original question, then, will be answered if we can find out whether virtue is knowledge or not.

By a brief argument on lines familiar from the *Protagoras*, Socrates convinces Meno that it is logical to identify virtue with knowledge. He now, however, raises a new difficulty himself. This may be right in theory, but does practical experience bear it out? If something so important can be imparted by teaching, presumably there exist teachers of it, and pupils learning it; but Socrates has never been able to find any. However, here, by great good fortune, comes Anytus. He is the kind of man who ought to be able to help us on this point.

There follows an interlude which contains the only reference in the dialogue to the Sophists as a class. In contrast to the part they play in the *Protagoras*, the introduction of their claims here comes simply as a short interruption of the main argument, which is resumed after dismissing them. The profession of the Sophists to teach *arete* is a subject which Plato has dealt with elsewhere, and here he is after something different. Socrates suggests to Anytus that perhaps they may find the teachers they are looking for in the Sophists. Anytus replies by abusing them as dishonest quacks, and takes his departure with a not very veiled threat against Socrates, whom he was before long to bring to trial.

Continuing their discussion, Socrates and Meno conclude that the position of the Sophists seems to be too dubious for them to be acclaimed with any confidence as real teachers of virtue. It is strange: there appear to be grounds for doubt whether in practice it ever is taught: perhaps there was a flaw in the theoretical proof. We said that because virtue always led to right conduct, it must be knowledge: but we may have been mistaken in overlooking the claims of right opinion, which so long as a man possesses it may serve him as well, for practical purposes, as knowledge in the full sense. By means of an illustration Socrates explains the difference between the two. Briefly, right opinion is something that you take on trust, and is converted into knowledge only when you have worked out the explanation for yourself and understand the reason why it is true. You then have it, as it were, no longer at second-hand, and true opinion is to be contrasted with knowledge as second-hand information (e.g. when somebody is told the way to Larissa) with direct experience (of the man who has traversed the road himself).

The defects of right opinion as opposed to knowledge are its instability and impermanence and its mysterious origin, which makes it sometimes impossible for one man to impart it to another. The point (familiar from the *Protagoras*) about great statesmen not being able to pass on their virtue to their sons is made once more, and Socrates concludes from it that what constitutes their virtue cannot after all be knowledge, but only this mysterious right opinion or conjecture, in fact a kind of intuition. That seems to put them in the same class with poets and seers as men who excel by a sort of divine inspiration. This then is the conclusion to which the discussion apparently leads, namely that virtue is not something imparted by teaching, but simply comes to a man 'by divine dispensation without taking thought'; but Socrates ends, as in the *Protagoras*, by repeating his warning that they cannot truly know how virtue is acquired without first going thoroughly into the question of its essential nature; and this they have not done. There is a long road still to travel, and Plato takes it in the *Republic*.

THE GEOMETRICAL EXPERIMENT
WITH MENO'S SLAVE

THE question that springs to the mind of most people on first reading this section of the dialogue is: has Socrates's interrogation been fairly conducted, and does it really prove what Socrates seems to think it does, namely the ante-natal existence of the soul, which, at least at the beginning, he seems to regard as bound up with the whole religious doctrine of immortality and reincarnation? If however we take the experiment in its context, it is a different question that is of immediate importance to Socrates. The experiment is introduced because the major discussion has been held up by Meno's employment of the eristic argument against the usefulness of pursuing any philosophic or scientific inquiry at all; and the essential thing is to show that the argument is not valid, but that it is worth while seeking knowledge of the nature of virtue, or anything else, which one does not possess at the moment.

Leaving then until later the question whether the acquisition of knowledge is in reality the recollection of truths known before birth, what has been achieved by the demonstration? By making the experiment under controlled conditions of his own choosing, Socrates has been able to construct a working model of his own method of discussion, which will give to Meno, who has up till now regarded it as a form of mental torment, an unmistakable impression of its advantages. With this in mind, he makes explicit references back to their own discussion, to show how it corresponds to the model and what stage in the Socratic process he and Meno have now reached.

The first stage is the confident assertion that comes from complete ignorance, mistaken by its possessor for knowledge. The slave says without hesitation that 'obviously' the double square will have a double side. Similarly Meno, when asked what virtue is, had said 'That's easy'. Socrates pauses (82E) to point out to Meno that this is the boy's condition, having selected a subject of inquiry in which Meno will have no difficulty in seeing at once not only the boy's conviction of knowledge but also his actual ignorance of the truth.

Next the boy is shown that his first answer was wrong, and is reduced to a helpless confession of ignorance (84A). Here Socrates breaks off again to make Meno admit that this is a better state than the first. In the controlled experiment that is obvious, though when the same technique was applied to Meno he had complained bitterly. Socrates refers explicitly to Meno's comparison of him to the sting-ray, and rallies him on his claim to have held forth admirably on virtue in the past. The value of the Socratic elenchus (as this part of the process is called) is that it (a) clears away the conceit of false knowledge and (b) instils the desire to learn as a natural consequence of coming to realize one's ignorance.

At this point in the main discussion, progress was barred by the eristic objection that no man can seek to find out something that he does not know, because he will have no means of recognizing it when found. In the experiment, the same point marks the beginning of the second phase of Socratic interrogation, the phase which entitles it to be called, as he calls it in the *Theatetus*, mental midwifery. His questions bring into the light of day ideas which were latent in the other's mind, or to use his own metaphor, they assist the delivery of ideas with which the other was pregnant. It is this positive stage that puts the greatest strain on a reader's credulity, at least if he is expected to regard it as proof that we unconsciously possess knowledge all the time, having acquired it in a previous, discarnate state. But we may fairly consider the following points:

1. In a way the slave did already possess the right answers somewhere in his mind, otherwise he could not have

given genuine assent to the alternative which at each stage Socrates puts before him – could not, as we should put it, have 'seen' that the suggested answer is right and others wrong. Even if we think Socrates's questions are blatantly leading, we must in fairness believe that the boy does do this, i.e. that he does not say yes simply to please Socrates, but because he realizes that it is the obvious answer. We may do so the more readily, because any person of ordinary intelligence would in fact realize it. What shows him his errors, and the right answers, is not so much Socrates's questions as the diagrams themselves. When the square on the three-foot side is drawn, he can see at once that it contains nine square feet, not eight. Similarly when the diagonals are drawn, he can see without Socrates telling him that the part cut off by each is the exact half of one of the squares. Moreover it would be possible, given time, for anyone to draw these diagrams, and learn the truth from them, for himself without an instructor. In his book *Before and after Socrates* Cornford quotes the anecdote about Pascal, whose father refused to allow him to learn geometry. (If not true, it is enough that it could be true.) In his own room, the boy drew figures on the floor with charcoal, without even knowing the proper names to apply to them, made out his own axioms and definitions, and had reached the thirty-second proposition of the first book of Euclid before he was discovered.

What the experiment teaches could be expressed as the difference between empirical and *a priori* knowledge, the one referring to the natural, changeable world in which we live, and the other to universal and timeless truths; and it suggests that whereas we have to learn facts of the former kind either from our own experience of the outside world or on the authority of another, the latter type of truth does seem in some way to come up from inside us so that we can work it out for ourselves. The date of a historical event, or the chemical formula for water, are things that we simply have to be told. Not so the truths of mathematics (nor, in

Plato's belief, of morals). No doubt the two halves of the
visible square, when Socrates had roughly sketched it out
with a stick in the sand and ploughed a diagonal across it,
were *not* precisely equal. Yet the slave replies with confidence – and this time rightly – that they are, because he
knows (without being told by anyone) that the question
refers not to this particular square but to the universal,
mathematical concept of a square. It is, as Plato would say,
a truth of the intelligible, not of the sensible world; and it is
this kind of truth that he conceives of as being acquired by
recollection. Mathematics in Greece, though elementary
compared with their modern counterpart, had advanced
sufficiently to make this duality plain to Plato. Today it is
even plainer: $\sqrt{-1}$ is something the like of which we never
meet in this world. Common-sense, and the elementary type
of mathematics that deals mostly in common-sense arguments, tells us that when a number is multiplied by itself
the product must always be positive, so that any square
number must be a positive and not a minus one. Yet mathe-
maticians work happily with the idea that -1 can have a
square root, and it yields them intelligible results. How do
we have any knowledge of $\sqrt{-1}$? Plato would say that
since it is not exemplified in anything that we experience
in this life, and is indeed contradicted by experience, we
must have encountered it among the eternal truths with
which our disembodied intelligence was face to face before
birth.

2. The educational value of the Socratic method should
also be appreciated. Whatever we may think about the
claim that the boy already had these right opinions about
geometry lying hidden in his mind before the conversation,
there is no doubt that they are genuinely his opinions now.
A less gifted, or less patient, teacher might say straight
away: 'Now learn this and don't forget it: to draw a square
double the size of a given square, you draw it on the diagonal of that square.' The pupil would dutifully repeat this,

but he would not *know* it in the sense in which Socrates (and we also) understand knowledge. Unless he can remember that particular sentence, he will forget the truth that it expresses, and in any case, if someone else tells him something different, he may as easily believe that. But the slave's opinion will not now be so easily shaken. Through the cross-questioning method he has seen for himself that it is so, almost as much as if, like the young Pascal, he had discovered it completely unaided. He has seen that neither a double side nor a side 1½ times as long gives the desired result, and he has a mental picture of how the true double square is built up from four half squares. He is on the way to being able to 'give an account', to explain and defend his beliefs. This is a lesson of permanent value for teachers, and it is still very imperfectly learned.

3. To appreciate the episode justly, we must also take into account Socrates's concluding words at 86 B,C. He clearly disclaims certainty for some of what he has been saying, though scholars have differed as to how much. There is no reason why we should not take his words at their face value. The one thing that he claims to feel sure of is that the eristic argument against inquiry is false. The quest for new knowledge is not a hopeless one, and to believe the contrary is positively harmful. So much he claims to have demonstrated, and the natural conclusion from his words is that he does not think he has substantiated either the full religious doctrine from which he set out – the priestly tale about immortality and reincarnation – or even the theory that learning is the recollection of ante-natal knowledge. This modest summing-up is more in accordance with our own impression of the experiment as well as being a justifiable inference from the words.

We must, however, beware of supposing that, if Plato is too clear a thinker to believe that what he has said here is full proof of the religious doctrines, therefore he did not believe them to be true. Other dialogues show that he took them seriously and was firmly convinced of the soul's immortality. The *Phaedo, Phaedrus*, and other works leave no reasonable doubt that he believed in the cycle of births as well. In the *Phaedo*, which there are good reasons for thinking was written later than the *Meno*, the theory of recollection is brought into connexion with immortality and used as a partial proof of it. Here on the other hand the point at issue is the practical one of showing that new knowledge can be acquired, and so allowing the main discussion about virtue to proceed. He has not yet satisfied himself as to the rational proofs of immortality, and puts off that problem to the time when he can devote a dialogue to it as his main topic.

4. One thing more should be noticed before we leave the experiment: that is, the first appearance of 'opinion' or 'belief' (Greek *doxa*) as an intermediate stage between sheer ignorance and knowledge, a conception which acquires great importance later in the dialogue. The eristic dilemma, like all dilemmas, presented a simple 'either-or'. It assumed only two alternatives: either one knows something or one does not. The recollection-theory evades it by recognizing a process, with several stages, between blank ignorance and complete knowledge. Blank ignorance indeed, in the sense that the mind is a complete *tabula rasa*, is something that we never suffer from. Not even at birth does it resemble a sheet of paper on which nothing has been written. Rather, we might say, there is writing on it in invisible ink which only needs the proper reagent to make it perceptible. Thus the true stages in the progress of knowledge are: (i) unconscious knowledge, (ii) opinion or belief, (iii) conversion of opinion into knowledge.

(i) The theory holds that knowledge of a certain kind may be present in our minds without our being consciously aware of it or having been aware of it since birth. The antecedent possibility of such a state of mind may be illustrated from the familiar experience of ordinary forgetfulness, as when we cannot say the name of an acquaintance yet know enough to reject wrong suggestions and recognize the right one when it is put to us. Plato's metaphor of mental 'pregnancy' and 'midwifery' refers to the same thing.

(ii) This unconscious knowledge when first awakened by questioning cannot yet be called knowledge in the full sense. Psychologically it is only opinion or belief (*doxa*). This word Plato, who avoids the precision of technical terms, uses in two different ways. In the first place it is an as yet imperfectly conscious and unco-ordinated cognition of the same eternal truths which are the objects of knowledge. This is the state of mind of the slave when Socrates has finished his questioning and so brought him to a 'true opinion' about a mathematical problem. The opinion is genuinely his own, as it would not have been had he simply been told the answer with the questioning process omitted; but it is not yet firmly and impregnably established in his mind as cognition must be to deserve the name of knowledge. So to establish it would necessitate several repetitions of the process. The difference is one of degree of cognition only; the object of cognition is the same whether it is opinion or knowledge.

In the second place *doxa* is applied by Plato to what we should call knowledge of the sensible world, including all natural science however securely based on inductive evidence or so-called laws of nature. In his view there can be no 'knowledge' of that, since the natural world is constantly changing. One of his criteria for knowledge is that it should be stable and lasting, which it can only be if its objects are stable and unchanging themselves. Concerning the changing world of experience, therefore, we can only have opinion or belief.

Besides the insecurity of opinion, another difference between the two is that our minds can contain false opinions, whereas knowledge must be true or it is not knowledge. The slave at first believed that the double square must have a double side. These false beliefs have to be disproved by being shown to be inconsistent with other beliefs that one is willing to accept as more certain. The problem of how the mind can entertain false beliefs is not here considered by Plato. He faces it in later dialogues, particularly the *Theaetetus* and *Sophist*.

(iii) Lastly comes the conversion of true opinion into knowledge. This, says Socrates, will happen in the case of the slave when he has been put through the demonstration many times and in different ways, until he carries immovably in his mind how each proposition necessarily follows from others which he has seen to be true. This is what is described later in the dialogue as 'tethering' or securing the opinion by a full working out of the reasons for it.

THE MENO

MENO. Can you tell me Socrates – is virtue something that
can be taught? Or does it come by practice? Or is it
neither teaching nor practice that gives it to a man but
natural aptitude or something else?

SOCRATES. Well Meno, in the old days the Thessalians had
a great reputation among the Greeks for their wealth and
their horsemanship. Now it seems they are philosophers
as well – especially the men of Larissa, where your friend
Aristippus comes from. It is Gorgias who has done it.
He went to that city and captured the hearts of the
foremost of the Aleuadae for his wisdom (among
them your own admirer Aristippus), not to speak
of other leading Thessalians. In particular he got you
into the habit of answering any question you might
be asked, with the confidence and dignity appropriate
to those who know the answers, just as he himself invites
questions of every kind from anyone in the Greek world
who wishes to ask, and never fails to answer them. But
here at Athens, my dear Meno, it is just the reverse.
There is a dearth of wisdom, and it looks as if it had
migrated from our part of the country to yours. At any
rate if you put your question to any of our people, they
will all alike laugh and say: 'You must think I am singu-
larly fortunate, to know whether virtue can be taught
or how it is acquired. The fact is that far from knowing
whether it can be taught, I have no idea what virtue
itself is.'

That is my own case. I share the poverty of my fellow-
countrymen in this respect, and confess to my shame that
I have no knowledge about virtue at all. And how can I
know a property of something when I don't even know

what it is? Do you suppose that somebody entirely ignorant who Meno is could say whether he is handsome and rich and well-born or the reverse? Is that possible, do you think?

MENO. No. But is this true about yourself, Socrates, that
C   you don't even know what virtue is? Is this the report that we are to take home about you?

SOCRATES. Not only that; you may say also that, to the best of my belief, I have never yet met anyone who did know.

MENO. What! Didn't you meet Gorgias when he was here?

SOCRATES. Yes.

MENO. And you still didn't think he knew?

SOCRATES. I'm a forgetful sort of person, and I can't say just now what I thought at the time. Probably he did know, and I expect you know what he used to say about
D   it. So remind me what it was, or tell me yourself if you will. No doubt you agree with him.

MENO. Yes I do.

SOCRATES. Then let's leave him out of it, since after all he isn't here. What do you yourself say virtue is? I do ask you in all earnestness not to refuse me, but to speak out. I shall be only too happy to be proved wrong if you and Gorgias turn out to know this, although I said I had never met anyone who did.

E   MENO. But there is no difficulty about it. First of all, if it is manly virtue you are after, it is easy to see that the virtue of a man consists in managing the city's affairs capably, and so that he will help his friends and injure his foes while taking care to come to no harm himself. Or if you want a woman's virtue, that is easily described. She must be a good housewife, careful with her stores and obedient to her husband. Then there is another virtue for a child, male or female, and another for an old man, free
72   or slave as you like; and a great many more kinds of virtue, so that no one need be at a loss to say what it is. For every act and every time of life, with reference to each

separate function, there is a virtue for each one of us, and similarly, I should say, a vice.

SOCRATES. I seem to be in luck. I wanted one virtue and I find that you have a whole swarm of virtues to offer. But seriously, to carry on this metaphor of the swarm, suppose I asked you what a bee is, what is its essential nature, B and you replied that bees were of many different kinds, what would you say if I went on to ask: 'And is it in being bees that they are many and various and different from one another? Or would you agree that it is not in this respect that they differ, but in something else, some other quality like size or beauty?'

MENO. I should say that in so far as they are bees, they don't differ from one another at all.

SOCRATES. Suppose I then continued: 'Well, this is just C what I want you to tell me. What is that character in respect of which they don't differ at all, but are all the same?' I presume you would have something to say?

MENO. I should.

SOCRATES. Then do the same with the virtues. Even if they are many and various, yet at least they all have some common character which makes them virtues. That is what ought to be kept in view by anyone who answers the question: 'What is virtue?' Do you follow me? D

MENO. I think I do, but I don't yet really grasp the question as I should wish.

SOCRATES. Well, does this apply in your mind only to virtue, that there is a different one for a man and a woman and the rest? Is it the same with health and size and strength, or has health the same character everywhere, if it is health, whether it be in a man or any other B creature?

MENO. I agree that health is the same in a man or in a woman.

SOCRATES. And what about size and strength? If a woman is strong, will it be the same thing, the same strength, that makes her strong? My meaning is that in its char-

acter as strength, it is no different, whether it be in a
man or in a woman. Or do you think it is?

MENO. No.

73 SOCRATES. And will virtue differ, in its character as virtue, whether it be in a child or an old man, a woman or a
man?

MENO. I somehow feel that this is not on the same level as
the other cases.

SOCRATES. Well then, didn't you say that a man's virtue
lay in directing the city well, and a woman's in directing
her household well?

MENO. Yes.

SOCRATES. And is it possible to direct anything well –
city or household or anything else – if not temperately
and justly?

B MENO. Certainly not.

SOCRATES. And that means with temperance and justice?

MENO. Of course.

SOCRATES. Then both man and woman need the same
qualities, justice and temperance, if they are going to be
good.

MENO. It looks like it.

SOCRATES. And what about your child and old man? Could
they be good if they were incontinent and unjust?

MENO. Of course not.

SOCRATES. They must be temperate and just?

MENO. Yes.

C SOCRATES. So everyone is good in the same way, since
they become good by possessing the same qualities.

MENO. So it seems.

SOCRATES. And if they did not share the same virtue, they
would not be good in the same way.

MENO. No.

SOCRATES. Seeing then that they all have the same virtue,
try to remember and tell me what Gorgias, and you who
share his opinion, say it is.

MENO. It must be simply the capacity to govern men, if you are looking for one quality to cover all the instances.   D

SOCRATES. Indeed I am. But does this virtue apply to a child or a slave? Should a slave be capable of governing his master, and if he does, is he still a slave?

MENO. I hardly think so.

SOCRATES. It certainly doesn't sound likely. And here is another point. You speak of 'capacity to govern'. Shall we not add 'justly but not otherwise'?

MENO. I think we should, for justice is virtue.

SOCRATES. Virtue, do you say, or *a* virtue?   E

MENO. What do you mean?

SOCRATES. Something quite general. Take roundness, for instance. I should say that it is a shape, not simply that it is shape, my reason being that there are other shapes as well.

MENO. I see your point, and I agree that there are other virtues besides justice.

SOCRATES. Tell me what they are. Just as I could name   74 other shapes if you told me to, in the same way mention some other virtues.

MENO. In my opinion then courage is a virtue and temperance and wisdom and dignity and many other things.

SOCRATES. This puts us back where we were. In a different way we have discovered a number of virtues when we were looking for one only. This single virtue, which permeates each of them, we cannot find.

MENO. No, I cannot yet grasp it as you want, a single virtue   B covering them all, as I do in other instances.

SOCRATES. I'm not surprised, but I shall do my best to get us a bit further if I can. You understand, I expect, that the question applies to everything. If someone took the example I mentioned just now, and asked you: 'What is shape?' and you replied that roundness is shape, and he then asked you as I did, 'Do you mean it is shape or *a* shape?' you would reply of course that it is *a* shape.

MENO. Certainly.

c SOCRATES. Your reason being that there are other shapes as well.

MENO. Yes.

SOCRATES. And if he went on to ask you what they were, you would tell him.

MENO. Yes.

SOCRATES. And the same with colour – if he asked you what it is, and on your replying 'White', took you up with: 'Is white colour or *a* colour?' you would say that it is *a* colour, because there are other colours as well.

MENO. I should.

D SOCRATES. And if he asked you to, you would mention other colours which are just as much colours as white is.

MENO. Yes.

SOCRATES. Suppose then he pursued the question as I did, and objected: 'We always arrive at a plurality, but that is not the kind of answer I want. Seeing that you call these many particulars by one and the same name, and say that every one of them is a shape, even though they are the contrary of each other, tell me what this is which embraces round as well as straight, and what you mean by

E shape when you say that straightness is a shape as much as roundness. You do say that?'

MENO. Yes.

SOCRATES. 'And in saying it, do you mean that roundness is no more round than straight, and straightness no more straight than round?'

MENO. Of course not.

SOCRATES. 'Yet you do say that roundness is no more a shape than straightness, and the other way about.'

MENO. Quite true.

SOCRATES. 'Then what is this thing which is called "shape"? Try to tell me.' If when asked this question

75 either about shape or colour you said: 'But I don't understand what you want, or what you mean', your questioner would perhaps be surprised and say: 'Don't you see that I am looking for what is the same in all of them?'

Would you even so be unable to reply, if the question was: 'What is it that is common to roundness and straightness and the other things which you call shapes?' Do your best to answer, as practice for the question about virtue.

MENO. No, you do it, Socrates.   B

SOCRATES. Do you want me to give in to you?

MENO. Yes.

SOCRATES. And will you in your turn give me an answer about virtue?

MENO. I will.

SOCRATES. In that case I must do my best. It's in a good cause.

MENO. Certainly.

SOCRATES. Well now, let's try to tell you what shape is. See if you accept this definition. Let us define it as the only thing which always accompanies colour. Does that satisfy you, or do you want it in some other way? I should be content if your definition of virtue were on similar lines.

MENO. But that's a naïve sort of definition, Socrates.   C

SOCRATES. How?

MENO. Shape, if I understand what you say, is what always accompanies colour. Well and good – but if somebody says that he doesn't know what colour is, but is no better off with it than he is with shape, what sort of answer have you given him, do you think?

SOCRATES. A true one; and if my questioner were one of the clever, disputatious and quarrelsome kind, I should say to him: 'You have heard my answer. If it is wrong, it   D is for you to take up the argument and refute it.' However, when friendly people, like you and me, want to converse with each other, one's reply must be milder and more conducive to discussion. By that I mean that it must not only be true, but must employ terms with which the questioner admits he is familiar. So I will try to answer you like that. Tell me therefore, whether you

recognize the term 'end'; I mean limit or boundary –
all these words I use in the same sense. Prodicus might
perhaps quarrel with us, but I assume you speak of
something being bounded or coming to an end. That
is all I mean, nothing subtle.

MENO. I admit the notion, and believe I understand your
meaning.

SOCRATES. And again, you recognize 'surface' and 'solid',
as they are used in geometry?

MENO. Yes.

SOCRATES. Then with these you should by this time understand my definition of shape. To cover all its instances,
I say that shape is that in which a solid terminates,
or more briefly, it is the limit of a solid.

MENO. And how do you define colour?

SOCRATES. What a shameless fellow you are, Meno. You
keep bothering an old man to answer, but refuse to exercise your memory and tell me what was Gorgias's definition of virtue.

MENO. I will, Socrates, as soon as you tell me this.

SOCRATES. Anyone talking to you could tell blindfold
that you are a handsome man and still have your admirers.

MENO. Why so?

SOCRATES. Because you are for ever laying down the law
as spoilt boys do, who act the tyrant as long as their
youth lasts. No doubt you have discovered that I can
never resist good looks. Well, I will give in and let you
have your answer.

MENO. Do by all means.

SOCRATES. Would you like an answer à la Gorgias, such as
you would most readily follow?

MENO. Of course I should.

SOCRATES. You and he believe in Empedocles's theory of
effluences, do you not?

MENO. Whole-heartedly.

SOCRATES. And passages to which and through which the
effluences make their way?

MENO. Yes.

SOCRATES. Some of the effluences fit into some of the passages, whereas others are too coarse or too fine.   D

MENO. That is right.

SOCRATES. Now you recognize the term 'sight'?

MENO. Yes.

SOCRATES. From these notions, then, 'grasp what I would tell', as Pindar says. Colour is an effluence from shapes commensurate with sight and perceptible by it.

MENO. That seems to me an excellent answer.

SOCRATES. No doubt it is the sort you are used to. And you probably see that it provides a way to define sound and smell and many similar things.

MENO. So it does.   E

SOCRATES. Yes, it's a high-sounding answer, so you like it better than the one on shape.

MENO. I do.

SOCRATES. Nevertheless, son of Alexidemus, I am convinced that the other is better; and I believe you would agree with me if you had not, as you told me yesterday, to leave before the mysteries, but could stay and be initiated.*

MENO. I would stay, Socrates, if you gave me more answers   77 like this.

SOCRATES. You may be sure I shan't be lacking in keenness to do so, both for your sake and mine; but I'm afraid I may not be able to do it often. However, now it is your turn to do as you promised, and try to tell me the general nature of virtue. Stop making many out of one, as the humorists say when somebody breaks a plate. Just leave virtue whole and sound and tell me what it is, as in the   B examples I have given you.

---

* Evidently the Athenians are about to celebrate the famous rites of the Eleusinian Mysteries, but Meno has to return to Thessaly before they fall due. Plato frequently plays upon the analogy between religious initiation, which bestowed a revelation of divine secrets, and the insight which comes from initiation into the truths of philosophy.

MENO. It seems to me then, Socrates, that virtue is, in the words of the poet, 'to rejoice in the fine and have power', and I define it as desiring fine things and being able to acquire them.

SOCRATES. When you speak of a man desiring fine things, do you mean it is good things he desires?

MENO. Certainly.

c SOCRATES. Then do you think some men desire evil and others good? Doesn't everyone, in your opinion, desire good things?

MENO. No.

SOCRATES. And would you say that the others suppose evils to be good, or do they still desire them although they recognize them as evil?

MENO. Both, I should say.

SOCRATES. What? Do you really think that anyone who recognizes evils for what they are, nevertheless desires them?

MENO. Yes.

SOCRATES. Desires in what way? To possess them?

D MENO. Of course.

SOCRATES. In the belief that evil things bring advantage to their possessor, or harm?

MENO. Some in the first belief, but some also in the second.

SOCRATES. And do you believe that those who suppose evil things bring advantage understand that they are evil?

MENO. No, that I can't really believe.

SOCRATES. Isn't it clear then that this class, who don't recognize evils for what they are, don't desire evil but
E what they think is good, though in fact it is evil; those who through ignorance mistake bad things for good obviously desire the good.

MENO. For them I suppose that is true.

SOCRATES. Now as for those whom you speak of as desiring evils in the belief that they do harm to their possessor, these presumably know that they will be injured by them?

MENO. They must.

SOCRATES. And don't they believe that whoever is injured 78
is, in so far as he is injured, unhappy?

MENO. That too they must believe.

SOCRATES. And unfortunate?

MENO. Yes.

SOCRATES. Well, does anybody want to be unhappy and
unfortunate?

MENO. I suppose not.

SOCRATES. Then if not, nobody desires what is evil; for
what else is unhappiness but desiring evil things and
getting them?

MENO. It looks as if you are right, Socrates, and nobody B
desires what is evil.

SOCRATES. Now you have just said that virtue consists in
a wish for good things plus the power to acquire them.
In this definition the wish is common to everyone, and in
that respect no one is better than his neighbour.

MENO. So it appears.

SOCRATES. So if one man is better than another, it must
evidently be in respect of the power, and virtue, according to your account, is the power of acquiring good
things. C

MENO. Yes, my opinion is exactly as you now express it.

SOCRATES. Let us see whether you have hit the truth this
time. You may well be right. The power of acquiring
good things, you say, is virtue?

MENO. Yes.

SOCRATES. And by good do you mean such things as
health and wealth?

MENO. I include the gaining both of gold and silver and of
high and honourable office in the State.

SOCRATES. Are these the only classes of goods that you
recognize?

MENO. Yes, I mean everything of that sort.

SOCRATES. Right. In the definition of Meno, hereditary D
guest-friend of the Great King, the acquisition of gold

and silver is virtue. Do you add 'just and righteous' to the word 'acquisition', or doesn't it make any difference to you? Do you call it virtue all the same even if they are unjustly acquired?

MENO. Certainly not.

SOCRATES. Vice then?

MENO. Most certainly.

SOCRATES. So it seems that justice or temperance or piety, or some other part of virtue, must attach to the acquisition. Otherwise, although it is a means to good things, it
B will not be virtue.

MENO. No, how could you have virtue without these?

SOCRATES. In fact lack of gold and silver, if it results from failure to acquire it – either for oneself or another – in circumstances which would have made its acquisition unjust, is itself virtue.

MENO. It would seem so.

SOCRATES. Then to have such goods is no more virtue than to lack them. Rather we may say that whatever is
79 accompanied by justice is virtue, whatever is without qualities of that sort is vice.

MENO. I agree that your conclusion seems inescapable.

SOCRATES. But a few minutes ago we called each of these – justice, temperance, and the rest – a part of virtue?

MENO. Yes, we did.

SOCRATES. So it seems you are making a fool of me.

MENO. How so, Socrates?

SOCRATES. I have just asked you not to break virtue up into fragments, and given you models of the type of answer I wanted, but taking no notice of this you tell me
B that virtue consists in the acquisition of good things with justice; and justice, you agree, is a part of virtue.

MENO. True.

SOCRATES. So it follows from your own statements that to act with a part of virtue is virtue, if you call justice and all the rest parts of virtue. The point I want to make is that whereas I asked you to give me an account of virtue as a whole, far from telling me what it is itself you say that every action is virtue which exhibits a part of virtue as if you had already told me what the whole is, so that I C should recognize it even if you chop it up into bits. It seems to me that we must put the same old question to you, my dear Meno – the question: 'What is virtue?' – if every act becomes virtue when combined with a part of virtue. That is, after all, what it means to say that every act performed with justice is virtue. Don't you agree that the same question needs to be put? Does anyone know what a part of virtue is, without knowing the whole?

MENO. I suppose not.

SOCRATES. No, and if you remember, when I replied to D you about shape just now, I believe we rejected the type of answer that employs terms which are still in question and not yet agreed upon.

MENO. We did, and rightly.

SOCRATES. Then please do the same. While the nature of virtue as a whole is still under question, don't suppose that you can explain it to anyone in terms of its parts, or E by any similar type of explanation. Understand rather that the same question remains to be answered; you say this and that about virtue, but what *is* it? Does this seem nonsense to you?

MENO. No, to me it seems right enough.

SOCRATES. Then go back to the beginning and answer my question. What do you and your friend say that virtue is?

MENO. Socrates, even before I met you they told me that in plain truth you are a perplexed man yourself and reduce 80 others to perplexity. At this moment I feel you are exercising magic and witchcraft upon me and positively laying me under your spell until I am just a mass of helplessness. If I may be flippant, I think that not only in outward appearance but in other respects as well you are exactly like the flat sting-ray that one meets in the sea. Whenever anyone comes into contact with it, it numbs him, and that is the sort of thing that you seem to be doing to me now. My mind and my lips are

B literally numb, and I have nothing to reply to you. Yet I have spoken about virtue hundreds of times, held forth often on the subject in front of large audiences, and very well too, or so I thought. Now I can't even say what it is. In my opinion you are well advised not to leave Athens and live abroad. If you behaved like this as a foreigner in another country, you would most likely be arrested as a wizard.

SOCRATES. You're a real rascal, Meno. You nearly took me in.

MENO. Just what do you mean?

C SOCRATES. I see why you used a simile about me.

MENO. Why, do you think?

SOCRATES. To be compared to something in return. All good-looking people, I know perfectly well, enjoy a game of comparisons. They get the best of it, for naturally handsome folk provoke handsome similes. But I'm not going to oblige you. As for myself, if the sting-ray paralyses others only through being paralysed itself, then the comparison is just, but not otherwise. It isn't that, knowing the answers myself, I perplex other people. The truth is rather that I infect them also with the per-

D plexity I feel myself. So with virtue now. I don't know what it is. You may have known before you came into contact with me, but now you look as if you don't. Nevertheless I am ready to carry out, together with you, a joint investigation and inquiry into what it is.

MENO. But how will you look for something when you don't in the least know what it is? How on earth are you going to set up something you don't know as the object of your search? To put it another way, even if you come right up against it, how will you know that what you have found is the thing you didn't know?

SOCRATES. I know what you mean. Do you realize that

E what you are bringing up is the trick argument that a man cannot try to discover either what he knows or what he does not know? He would not seek what he knows, for since he knows it there is no need of the inquiry, nor what he does not know, for in that case he does not even know what he is to look for.

MENO. Well, do you think it a good argument?   81

SOCRATES. No.

MENO. Can you explain how it fails?

SOCRATES. I can. I have heard from men and women who understand the truths of religion –

[*Here he presumably pauses to emphasize the solemn change of tone which the dialogue undergoes at this point.*]

MENO. What did they say?

SOCRATES. Something true, I thought, and fine.

MENO. What was it, and who were they?

SOCRATES. Those who tell it are priests and priestesses of the sort who make it their business to be able to account for the functions which they perform. Pindar speaks of it too, and many another of the poets who are divinely inspired. What they say is this – see whether you think they are speaking the truth. They say that the soul of man is immortal: at one time it comes to an end – that which is called death – and at another is born again, but is never finally exterminated. On these grounds a man must live all his days as righteously as possible. For those from whom

> Persephone receives requital for ancient doom,
> In the ninth year she restores again
> Their souls to the sun above.
> From whom rise noble kings   C
> And the swift in strength and greatest in wisdom;
> And for the rest of time
> They are called heroes and sanctified by men.*

Thus the soul, since it is immortal and has been born many times, and has seen all things both here and in the other world, has learned everything that is. So we need

* The quotation is from Pindar.

not be surprised if it can recall the knowledge of virtue or anything else which, as we see, it once possessed. All nature is akin, and the soul has learned everything, so that when a man has recalled a single piece of knowledge – *learned* it, in ordinary language – there is no reason why he should not find out all the rest, if he keeps a stout heart and does not grow weary of the search; for seeking and learning are in fact nothing but recollection.

We ought not then to be led astray by the contentious argument you quoted. It would make us lazy, and is music in the ears of weaklings. The other doctrine produces energetic seekers after knowledge; and being convinced of its truth, I am ready, with your help, to inquire into the nature of virtue.

MENO. I see, Socrates. But what do you mean when you say that we don't learn anything, but that what we call learning is recollection? Can you teach me that it is so?

SOCRATES. I have just said that you're a rascal, and now you ask me if I can teach you, when I say there is no such thing as teaching, only recollection. Evidently you want to catch me contradicting myself straight away.

MENO. No, honestly, Socrates, I wasn't thinking of that. It was just habit. If you can in any way make clear to me that what you say is true, please do.

SOCRATES. It isn't an easy thing, but still I should like to do what I can since you ask me. I see you have a large number of retainers here. Call one of them, anyone you like, and I will use him to demonstrate it to you.

MENO. Certainly. (*To a slave-boy.*) Come here.

SOCRATES. He is a Greek and speaks our language?

MENO. Indeed yes – born and bred in the house.

SOCRATES. Listen carefully then, and see whether it seems to you that he is learning from me or simply being reminded.

MENO. I will.

SOCRATES. Now boy, you know that a square is a figure like this?

(Socrates begins to draw figures in the sand at his feet. He points to the square ABCD.)

BOY. Yes.

SOCRATES. It has all these four sides equal?

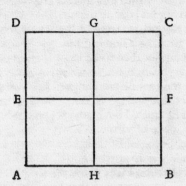

BOY. Yes.

SOCRATES. And these lines which go through the middle of it are also equal? (The lines EF, GH.)

BOY. Yes.

SOCRATES. Such a figure could be either larger or smaller, could it not?

BOY. Yes.

SOCRATES. Now if this side is two feet long, and this side the same, how many feet will the whole be? Put it this way. If it were two feet in this direction and only one in that, must not the area be two feet taken once?

BOY. Yes.

SOCRATES. But since it is two feet this way also, does it not become twice two feet?

BOY. Yes.

SOCRATES. And how many feet is twice two? Work it out and tell me.

BOY. Four.

SOCRATES. Now could one draw another figure double the size of this, but similar, that is, with all its sides equal like this one?

BOY. Yes.

SOCRATES. How many feet will its area be?

BOY. Eight.

SOCRATES. Now then, try to tell me how long each of its
E   sides will be. The present figure has a side of two feet. What will be the side of the double-sized one?

BOY. It will be double, Socrates, obviously.

SOCRATES. You see, Meno, that I am not teaching him anything, only asking. Now he thinks he knows the length of the side of the eight-feet square.

MENO. Yes.

SOCRATES. But does he?

MENO. Certainly not.

SOCRATES. He thinks it is twice the length of the other.

MENO. Yes.

SOCRATES. Now watch how he recollects things in order – the proper way to recollect.

You say that the side of double length produces the
83   double-sized figure? Like this I mean, not long this way and short that. It must be equal on all sides like the first figure, only twice its size, that is eight feet. Think a moment whether you still expect to get it from doubling the side.

BOY. Yes, I do.

SOCRATES. Well now, shall we have a line double the length of this (AB) if we add another the same length at this end (BJ)?

BOY. Yes.

B   SOCRATES. It is on this line then, according to you, that we shall make the eight-feet square, by taking four of the same length?

BOY. Yes.

SOCRATES. Let us draw in four equal lines (*i.e. counting* AJ, *and adding* JK, KL, *and* LA *made complete by drawing in its second half* LD), using the first as a base. Does this not give us what you call the eight-feet figure?

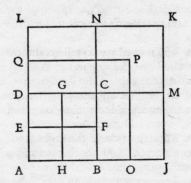

BOY. Certainly.

SOCRATES. But does it contain these four squares, each equal to the original four-feet one?

> (*Socrates has drawn in the lines* CM, CN *to complete the squares that he wishes to point out.*)

BOY. Yes.

SOCRATES. How big is it then? Won't it be four times as big?

BOY. Of course.

SOCRATES. And is four times the same as twice?

BOY. Of course not.

SOCRATES. So doubling the side has given us not a double c
but a fourfold figure?

BOY. True.

SOCRATES. And four times four are sixteen, are they not?

BOY. Yes.

SOCRATES. Then how big is the side of the eight-feet figure? This one has given us four times the original area, hasn't it?

BOY. Yes.

SOCRATES. And a side half the length gave us a square of four feet?

BOY. Yes.

SOCRATES. Good. And isn't a square of eight feet double this one and half that?

BOY. Yes.

D SOCRATES. Will it not have a side greater than this one but less than that?

BOY. I think it will.

SOCRATES. Right. Always answer what you think. Now tell me: was not this side two feet long, and this one four?

BOY. Yes.

SOCRATES. Then the side of the eight-feet figure must be longer than two feet but shorter than four?

BOY. It must.

E SOCRATES. Try to say how long you think it is.

BOY. Three feet.

SOCRATES. If so, shall we add half of this bit (BO, *half of* BJ) and make it three feet? Here are two, and this is one, and on this side similarly we have two plus one; and here is the figure you want.

(*Socrates completes the square* AOPQ.)

BOY. Yes.

SOCRATES. If it is three feet this way and three that, will the whole area be three times three feet?

BOY. It looks like it.

SOCRATES. And that is how many?

BOY. Nine.

SOCRATES. Whereas the square double our first square had to be how many?

BOY. Eight.

SOCRATES. But we haven't yet got the square of eight feet even from a three-feet side?

BOY. No.

SOCRATES. Then what length will give it? Try to tell us
84   exactly. If you don't want to count it up, just show us on the diagram.

BOY. It's no use, Socrates, I just don't know.

SOCRATES. Observe, Meno, the stage he has reached on the path of recollection. At the beginning he did not know the side of the square of eight feet. Nor indeed does he know it now, but then he thought he knew it and answered boldly, as was appropriate – he felt no perplexity. Now however he does feel perplexed. Not only does he not know the answer; he doesn't even think he knows.

MENO. Quite true.   B

SOCRATES. Isn't he in a better position now in relation to what he didn't know?

MENO. I admit that too.

SOCRATES. So in perplexing him and numbing him like the sting-ray, have we done him any harm?

MENO. I think not.

SOCRATES. In fact we have helped him to some extent towards finding out the right answer, for now not only is he ignorant of it but he will be quite glad to look for it. Up to now, he thought he could speak well and fluently, on many occasions and before large audiences, on the subject of a square double the size of a given square, maintaining that it must have a side of double the   C
length.

MENO. No doubt.

SOCRATES. Do you suppose then that he would have attempted to look for, or learn, what he thought he knew (though he did not), before he was thrown into perplexity, became aware of his ignorance, and felt a desire to know?

MENO. No.

SOCRATES. Then the numbing process was good for him?

MENO. I agree.

SOCRATES. Now notice what, starting from this state of perplexity, he will discover by seeking the truth in company with me, though I simply ask him questions with-   D
out teaching him. Be ready to catch me if I give him any

instruction or explanation instead of simply interrogating him on his own opinions.

(Socrates here rubs out the previous figures and starts again.)

Tell me, boy, is not this our square of four feet? (ABCD.) You understand?

BOY. Yes.

SOCRATES. Now we can add another equal to it like this? (BCEF.)

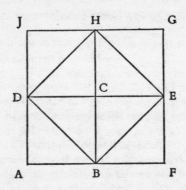

BOY. Yes.

SOCRATES. And a third here, equal to each of the others? (CEGH.)

BOY. Yes.

SOCRATES. And then we can fill in this one in the corner? (DCHJ.)

B BOY. Yes.

SOCRATES. Then here we have four equal squares?

BOY. Yes.

SOCRATES. And how many times the size of the first square is the whole?

BOY. Four times.

SOCRATES. And we want one double the size. You remember?

BOY. Yes.

SOCRATES. Now does this line going from corner to corner 85 cut each of these squares in half?

BOY. Yes.

SOCRATES. And these are four equal lines enclosing this area? (BEHD.)

BOY. They are.

SOCRATES. Now think. How big is this area?

BOY. I don't understand.

SOCRATES. Here are four squares. Has not each line cut off the inner half of each of them?

BOY. Yes.

SOCRATES. And how many such halves are there in this figure? (BEHD.)

BOY. Four.

SOCRATES. And how many in this one? (ABCD.)

BOY. Two.

SOCRATES. And what is the relation of four to two?

BOY. Double.

SOCRATES. How big is this figure then? B

BOY. Eight feet.

SOCRATES. On what base?

BOY. This one.

SOCRATES. The line which goes from corner to corner of the square of four feet?

BOY. Yes.

SOCRATES. The technical name for it is 'diagonal'; so if we use that name, it is your personal opinion that the square on the diagonal of the original square is double its area.

BOY. That is so, Socrates.

SOCRATES. What do you think, Meno? Has he answered with any opinions that were not his own?

MENO. No, they were all his. C

SOCRATES. Yet he did not know, as we agreed a few minutes ago.

MENO. True.

SOCRATES. But these opinions were somewhere in him, were they not?

MENO. Yes.

SOCRATES. So a man who does not know has in himself true opinions on a subject without having knowledge.

MENO. It would appear so.

SOCRATES. At present these opinions, being newly aroused, have a dream-like quality. But if the same questions are put to him on many occasions and in different ways, you can see that in the end he will have a know-
D ledge on the subject as accurate as anybody's.

MENO. Probably.

SOCRATES. This knowledge will not come from teaching but from questioning. He will recover it for himself.

MENO. Yes.

SOCRATES. And the spontaneous recovery of knowledge that is in him is recollection, isn't it?

MENO. Yes.

SOCRATES. Either then he has at some time acquired the knowledge which he now has, or he has always possessed it. If he always possessed it, he must always have known; if on the other hand he acquired it at some prev-
E ious time, it cannot have been in this life, unless somebody has taught him geometry. He will behave in the same way with all geometrical knowledge, and every other subject. Has anyone taught him all these? You ought to know, especially as he has been brought up in your household.

MENO. Yes, I know that no one ever taught him.

SOCRATES. And has he these opinions, or hasn't he?

MENO. It seems we can't deny it.

SOCRATES. Then if he did not acquire them in this life,
86 isn't it immediately clear that he possessed and had learned them during some other period?

MENO. It seems so.

SOCRATES. When he was not in human shape?

MENO. Yes.

SOCRATES. If then there are going to exist in him, both while he is and while he is not a man, true opinions which can be aroused by questioning and turned into knowledge, may we say that his soul has been for ever in a state of knowledge? Clearly he always either is or is not a man.

MENO. Clearly.

SOCRATES. And if the truth about reality is always in our soul, the soul must be immortal, and one must take courage and try to discover – that is, to recollect – what one doesn't happen to know, or (more correctly) remember, at the moment.

MENO. Somehow or other I believe you are right.

SOCRATES. I think I am. I shouldn't like to take my oath on the whole story, but one thing I am ready to fight for as long as I can, in word and act: that is, that we shall be better, braver and more active men if we believe it right to look for what we don't know than if we believe there is no point in looking because what we don't know we can never discover.

MENO. There too I am sure you are right.

SOCRATES. Then since we are agreed that it is right to inquire into something that one does not know, are you ready to face with me the question: what is virtue?

MENO. Quite ready. All the same, I would rather consider the question as I put it at the beginning, and hear your views on it; that is, are we to pursue virtue as something that can be taught, or do men have it as a gift of nature or how?

SOCRATES. If I were your master as well as my own, Meno, we should not have inquired whether or not virtue can be taught until we had first asked the main question – what it is; but not only do you make no attempt to govern your own actions – you prize your freedom, I suppose – but you attempt to govern mine. And you succeed too, so I shall let you have your way. There's nothing else for it, and it seems we must inquire into a single property of something about whose essential nature we are still in the dark. Just grant me one small relaxation of your sway, and allow me, in considering whether or not it can be taught, to make use of a hypothesis – the sort of thing, I mean, that geometers often use in their inquiries. When they are asked, for example, about a given area, whether it is possible for this area to be inscribed as a triangle in a given circle, they will probably reply: 'I don't know yet whether it fulfils the conditions, but I think I have a hypothesis which will help us in the matter. It is this. If the area is such that, when one has applied it [*sc. as a rectangle*] to the given line [*i.e. the diameter*] of the circle, it is deficient by another rectangle similar to the one which is applied, then, I should say, one result follows; if not, the result is different. If you ask me, then, about the inscription of the figure in the circle – whether it is possible or not – I am ready to answer you in this hypothetical way.'*

Let us do the same about virtue. Since we don't know what it is or what it resembles, let us use a hypothesis in investigating whether it is teachable or not. We shall say: 'What attribute of the soul must virtue be, if it is to be teachable or otherwise?' Well, in the first place, if it is anything else but knowledge, is there a possibility of anyone teaching it – or, in the language we used just now, reminding someone of it? We needn't worry about which name we are to give to the process, but simply ask: will it be teachable? Isn't it plain to everyone that a man is not taught anything except knowledge?

MENO. That would be my view.

---

* The geometrical illustration here adduced by Socrates is very loosely and obscurely expressed. Sir Thomas Heath in his *History of Greek Mathematics* (1921, vol. i, p. 298) says that C. Blass, writing in 1861, already knew of thirty different interpretations, and that many more had appeared since then. Fortunately it is not necessary to understand the example in order to grasp the hypothetical method which Socrates is expounding.

SOCRATES. If on the other hand virtue is some sort of knowledge, clearly it could be taught.

MENO. Certainly.

SOCRATES. So that question is easily settled; I mean, on what condition virtue would be teachable.

MENO. Yes.

SOCRATES. The next point then, I suppose, is to find out whether virtue is knowledge or something different.

MENO. That is the next question, I agree.   D

SOCRATES. Well then, do we assert that virtue is something good? Is that assumption a firm one for us?

MENO. Undoubtedly.

SOCRATES. That being so, if there exists any good thing different from, and not associated with, knowledge, virtue will not necessarily be any form of knowledge. If on the other hand knowledge embraces everything that is good, we shall be right to suspect that virtue is knowledge.

MENO. Agreed.

SOCRATES. First then is it virtue which makes us good?

MENO. Yes.

SOCRATES. And if good, then advantageous. All good   E things are advantageous, are they not?

MENO. Yes.

SOCRATES. So virtue itself must be something advantageous?

MENO. That follows also.

SOCRATES. Now suppose we consider what are the sort of things that profit us. Take them in a list. Health, we may say, and strength and good looks, and wealth – these and their like we call advantageous, you agree?

MENO. Yes.

SOCRATES. Yet we also speak of these things as sometimes   88 doing harm. Would you object to that statement?

MENO. No, it is so.

SOCRATES. Now look here: what is the controlling factor which determines whether each of these is advantageous or harmful? Isn't it right use which makes them advantageous, and lack of it, harmful?

MENO. Certainly.

SOCRATES. We must also take spiritual qualities into consideration. You recognize such things as temperance, justice, courage, quickness of mind, memory, nobility of character and others?

B MENO. Yes of course I do.

SOCRATES. Then take any such qualities which in your view are not knowledge but something different. Don't you think they may be harmful as well as advantageous? Courage for instance, if it is something thoughtless, just a sort of confidence. Isn't it true that to be confident without reason does a man harm, whereas a reasoned confidence profits him?

MENO. Yes.

SOCRATES. Temperance and quickness of mind are no different. Learning and discipline are profitable in conjunction with wisdom, but without it harmful.

C MENO. That is emphatically true.

SOCRATES. In short, everything that the human spirit undertakes or suffers will lead to happiness when it is guided by wisdom, but to the opposite, when guided by folly.

MENO. A reasonable conclusion.

SOCRATES. If then virtue is an attribute of the spirit, and one which cannot fail to be beneficial, it must be wisdom; for all spiritual qualities in and by themselves are neither advantageous nor harmful, but become advantageous or

D harmful by the presence with them of wisdom or folly. If we accept this argument, then virtue, to be something advantageous, must be a sort of wisdom.

MENO. I agree.

SOCRATES. To go back to the other class of things, wealth and the like, of which we said just now that they are sometimes good and sometimes harmful, isn't it the same with them? Just as wisdom when it governs our other psychological impulses turns them to advantage, and folly turns them to harm, so the mind by its right use and control of these material assets makes them profitable and by wrong use renders them harmful. **B**

MENO. Certainly.

SOCRATES. And the right user is the mind of the wise man, the wrong user the mind of the foolish.

MENO. That is so.

SOCRATES. So we may say in general that the goodness of non-spitirual assets depends on our spiritual character, and the goodness of that on wisdom. This argument **89** shows that the advantageous element must be wisdom; and virtue, we agree, is advantageous, so that amounts to saying that virtue is wisdom, either the whole or a part of it.

MENO. The argument seems to me fair enough.

SOCRATES. If so, good men cannot be good by nature.

MENO. I suppose not.

SOCRATES. There is another point. If they were, there **B** would probably be experts among us who could recognize the naturally good at an early stage. They would point them out to us and we should take them and shut them away safely in the Acropolis, sealing them up more carefully than bullion to protect them from corruption and ensure that when they came to maturity they would be of use to the State.

MENO. It would be likely enough.

SOCRATES. Since then goodness does not come by nature, is it got by learning? **C**

MENO. I don't see how we can escape the conclusion. Indeed it is obvious on our assumption that, if virtue is knowledge, it is teachable.

SOCRATES. I suppose so. But I wonder if we were right to bind ourselves to that.

MENO. Well, it seemed all right just now.

SOCRATES. Yes, but to be sound it has got to seem all right not only 'just now' but at this moment and in the future.

D   MENO. Of course. But what has occurred to you to make you turn against it and suspect that virtue may not be knowledge?

SOCRATES. I'll tell you. I don't withdraw from the position that if it is knowledge, it must be teachable; but as for its being knowledge, see whether you think my doubts on this point are well founded. If anything – not virtue only – is a possible subject of instruction, must there not be teachers and students of it?

B   MENO. Surely.

SOCRATES. And what of the converse, that if there are neither teachers nor students of a subject, we may safely infer that it cannot be taught?

MENO. That is true. But don't you think there are teachers of virtue?

SOCRATES. All I can say is that I have often looked to see if there are any, and in spite of all my efforts I cannot find them, though I have had plenty of fellow-searchers, the kind of men especially whom I believe to have most experience in such matters. But look Meno, here's a piece
90 of luck. Anytus has just sat down beside us. We couldn't do better than make him a partner in our inquiry. In the first place he is the son of Anthemion, a man of property and good sense, who didn't get his money out of the blue or as a gift – like Ismenias of Thebes who has just come into the fortune of a Croesus – but earned it by his own brains and hard work. Besides this he shows himself a decent, modest citizen with no arrogance or bombast or offensiveness about him. Also he brought up his son well and had him properly educated, as the Athenian people appreciate: look how they elect him into the highest offices in the State. This is certainly the right sort of man with whom to inquire whether there are any teachers of virtue, and if so who they are.

Please help us, Anytus – Meno, who is a friend of your family, and myself – to find out who may be the teachers of this subject. Look at it like this. If we wanted Meno to

become a good doctor, shouldn't we send him to the c
doctors to be taught?

ANYTUS. Of course.

SOCRATES. And if we wanted him to become a shoemaker,
to the shoemakers?

ANYTUS. Yes.

SOCRATES. And so on with other trades?

ANYTUS. Yes.

SOCRATES. Now another relevant question. When we
say that to make Meno a doctor we should be right in
sending him to the doctors, have we in mind that the
sensible thing is to send him to those who profess the D
subject rather than to those who don't, men who charge
a fee as professionals, having announced that they
are prepared to teach whoever likes to come and
learn?

ANYTUS. Yes.

SOCRATES. The same is surely true of flute-playing and
other accomplishments. If you want to make someone a
performer on the flute it would be very foolish to refuse E
to send him to those who undertake to teach the art and
are paid for it, but to go and bother other people instead
and have him try to learn from them – people who don't
set up to be teachers or take any pupils in the subject
which we want our young man to learn. Doesn't that
sound very unreasonable?

ANYTUS. Sheer stupidity I should say.

SOCRATES. I agree. And now we can both consult together about our visitor Meno. He has been telling me 91
all this while that he longs to acquire the kind of wisdom
and virtue which fits men to manage an estate or govern
a city, to look after their parents, and to entertain and
send off guests in proper style, both their own countrymen and foreigners. With this in mind, to whom would B
it be right to send him? What we have just said seems to
show that the right people are those who profess to be
teachers of virtue and offer their services freely to any

Greek who wishes to learn, charging a fixed fee for their instruction.

ANYTUS. Whom do you mean by that, Socrates?

SOCRATES. Surely you know yourself that they are the men called Sophists.

C ANYTUS. Good heavens, what a thing to say! I hope no relative of mine or any of my friends, Athenian or foreign, would be so mad as to go and let himself be ruined by those people. That's what they are, the manifest ruin and corruption of anyone who comes into contact with them.

SOCRATES. What, Anytus? Can they be so different from other claimants to useful knowledge that they not only don't do good, like the rest, to the material that one puts

D in their charge, but on the contrary spoil it – and have the effrontery to take money for doing so? I for one find it difficult to believe you. I know that one of them alone, Protagoras, earned more money from being a Sophist than an outstandingly fine craftsman like Phidias and ten other sculptors put together. A man who mends old shoes or restores coats couldn't get away with it for a

E month if he gave them back in worse condition than he received them; he would soon find himself starving. Surely it is incredible that Protagoras took in the whole of Greece, corrupting his pupils and sending them away worse than when they came to him, for more than forty years. I believe he was nearly seventy when he died, and had been practising for forty years, and all that time – indeed to this very day – his reputation has been consist-

92 ently high; and there are plenty of others besides Protagoras, some before his time and others still alive. Are we to suppose from your remark that they consciously deceive and ruin young men, or are they unaware of it themselves? Can these remarkably clever men – as some regard them – be mad enough for that?

ANYTUS. Far from it, Socrates. It isn't they who are mad, but rather the young men who hand over their money, and those responsible for them, who let them get into the Sophists' hands, are even worse. Worst of all are the B cities who allow them in, or don't expel them, whether it be a foreigner or one of themselves who tries that sort of game.

SOCRATES. Has one of the Sophists done you a personal injury, or why are you so hard on them?

ANYTUS. Heavens, no! I've never in my life had anything to do with a single one of them, nor would I hear of any of my family doing so.

SOCRATES. So you've had no experience of them at all?

ANYTUS. And don't want any either. C

SOCRATES. You surprise me. How can you know what is good or bad in something when you have no experience of it?

ANYTUS. Quite easily. At any rate I know *their* kind, whether I've had experience or not.

SOCRATES. It must be second sight, I suppose; for how else you know about them, judging from what you tell me yourself, I can't imagine. However, we are not asking whose instruction it is that would ruin Meno's char- D acter. Let us say that those are the Sophists if you like, and tell us instead about the ones we want. You can do a good turn to a friend of your father's house if you will let him know to whom in our great city he should apply for proficiency in the kind of virtue I have just described.

ANYTUS. Why not tell him yourself?

SOCRATES. Well, I did mention the men who in my opinion teach these things, but apparently I was talking nonsense. So you say, and you may well be right. Now it is E your turn to direct him; mention the name of any Athenian you like.

ANYTUS. But why mention a particular individual? Any decent Athenian gentleman whom he happens to meet, if he follows his advice, will make him a better man than the Sophists would.

SOCRATES. And did these gentlemen get their fine qualities

93 spontaneously – self-taught, as it were, and yet able to teach this untaught virtue to others?

ANYTUS. I suppose they in their turn learned it from forebears who were gentlemen like themselves. Would you deny that there have been many good men in our city?

SOCRATES. On the contrary, there are plenty of good statesmen here in Athens and have been as good in the past. The question is, have they also been good teachers of their own virtue? That is the point we are discussing now – not whether or not there are good men in Athens

B or whether there have been in past times, but whether virtue can be taught. It amounts to the question whether the good men of this and former times have known how to hand on to someone else the goodness that was in themselves, or whether on the contrary it is not something that can be handed over, or that one man can receive from another. That is what Meno and I have long been puzzling over. Look at it from your own point of

C view. You would say that Themistocles was a good man?

ANYTUS. Yes, none better.

SOCRATES. And that he, if anyone, must have been a good teacher of his own virtue?

ANYTUS. I suppose so, if he wanted to be.

SOCRATES. But don't you think he must have wanted others to become worthy men – above all, surely, his own son? Do you suppose he grudged him this and pur-

D posely didn't pass on his own virtue to him? You must have heard that he had his son Cleophantus so well trained in horsemanship that he could stand upright on horseback and throw a javelin from that position; and many other wonderful accomplishments the young man had, for his father had him taught and made expert in every skill that a good instructor could impart. You must have heard this from older people?

ANYTUS. Yes.

SOCRATES. No one, then, could say that there was anything wrong with the boy's natural powers?

ANYTUS. Perhaps not.   E

SOCRATES. But have you ever heard anyone, young or old,
say that Cleophantus the son of Themistocles was a good
and wise man in the way that his father was?

ANYTUS. Certainly not.

SOCRATES. Must we conclude then that Themistocles's
aim was to educate his son in other accomplishments, but
not to make him any better than his neighbours in his
own type of wisdom – that is, supposing that virtue
could be taught?

ANYTUS. I hardly think we can.

SOCRATES. So much then for Themistocles as a teacher of
virtue, whom you yourself agree to have been one of the
best men of former times. Take another example, Arist-   94
ides son of Lysimachus. You accept him as a good man?

ANYTUS. Surely.

SOCRATES. He too gave his son Lysimachus the best education in Athens, in all subjects where a teacher could
help; but did he make him a better man than his neighbour? You know him, I think, and can say what he is
like. Or again there is Pericles, that great and wise man.   B
He brought up two sons, Paralus and Xanthippus, and
had them taught riding, music, athletics, and all the other
skilled pursuits till they were as good as any in Athens.
Did he then not want to make them good men? Yes, he
wanted that, no doubt, but I am afraid it is something
that cannot be done by teaching. And in case you should
think that only very few, and those the most insignificant,   C
lacked this power, consider that Thucydides also had
two sons, Melesias and Stephanus, to whom he gave an
excellent education. Among other things they were the
best wrestlers in Athens, for he gave one to Xanthias to
train and the other to Eudoxus – the two who, I understand, were considered the finest wrestlers of their time.
You remember?

ANYTUS. I have heard of them.

SOCRATES. Surely then he would never have had his child-

PLATO

D ren taught these expensive pursuits and yet refused to
teach them to be good men – which would have cost
nothing at all – if virtue could have been taught? You
are not going to tell me that Thucydides was a man of no
account, or that he had not plenty of friends both at
Athens and among the allies? He came of an influential
family and was a great power both here and in the rest of
Greece. If virtue could have been taught, he would have
found the man to make his sons good, either among our
E own citizens or abroad, supposing his political duties
left him no time to do it himself. No, my dear Anytus,
it looks as if it cannot be taught.

ANYTUS. You seem to me, Socrates, to be too ready to run
people down. My advice to you, if you will listen to it,
is to be careful. I dare say that in all cities it is easier to do
95 a man harm than good, and it is certainly so here, as I
expect you know yourself.

SOCRATES. Anytus seems angry, Meno, and I am not surprised. He thinks I am slandering our statesmen, and
moreover he believes himself to be one of them. He
doesn't know what slander really is: if he ever finds out
he will forgive me.

However, tell me this yourself: are there not similar
fine characters in your country?

MENO. Yes certainly.

B SOCRATES. Do they come forward of their own accord to
teach the young? Do they agree that they are teachers
and that virtue can be taught?

MENO. No indeed, they don't agree on it at all. Sometimes
you will hear them say that it can be taught, sometimes
that it cannot.

SOCRATES. Ought we then to class as teachers of it men
who are not even agreed that it can be taught?

MENO. Hardly, I think.

SOCRATES. And what about the Sophists, the only people
C who profess to teach it? Do you think they do?

MENO. The thing I particularly admire about Gorgias, Socrates, is that you will never hear him make this claim; indeed he laughs at the others when he hears them do so. In his view his job is to make clever speakers.

SOCRATES. So you too don't think the Sophists are teachers?

MENO. I really can't say. Like most people I waver – sometimes I think they are and sometimes I think they are not.

SOCRATES. Has it ever occurred to you that you and our statesmen are not alone in this? The poet Theognis likewise says in one place that virtue is teachable and in another that it is not.

MENO. Really? Where?

SOCRATES. In the elegiacs in which he writes:

> *Eat, drink, and sit with men of power and weight,*
> *Nor scorn to gain the favour of the great.*
> *For fine men's teaching to fine ways will win thee:*
> *Low company destroys what wit is in thee.*

There he speaks as if virtue can be taught, doesn't he?

MENO. Clearly.

SOCRATES. But elsewhere he changes his ground a little

> *Were mind by art created and instilled*
> *Immense rewards had soon the pockets filled*

of the people who could do this. Moreover

> *No good man's son would ever worthless be,*
> *Taught by wise counsel. But no teacher's skill*
> *Can turn to good what is created ill.*

Do you see how he contradicts himself?

MENO. Plainly.

SOCRATES. Can you name any other subject, in which the professed teachers are not only not recognized as teachers of others, but are thought to have no understanding of it themselves, and to be no good at the very subject they profess to teach; whereas those who are acknowledged to be the best at it are in two minds whether it can be taught or not? When people are so confused about a subject, can you say that they are in a true sense teachers?

MENO. Certainly not.

SOCRATES. Well, if neither the Sophists nor those who display fine qualities themselves are teachers of virtue, I am
C   sure no one else can be, and if there are no teachers, there can be no students either.

MENO. I quite agree.

SOCRATES. And we have also agreed that a subject of which there were neither teachers nor students was not one which could be taught.

MENO. That is so.

SOCRATES. Now there turn out to be neither teachers nor students of virtue, so it would appear that virtue cannot be taught.

D MENO. So it seems, if we have made no mistake; and it makes me wonder, Socrates, whether there are in fact no good men at all, or how they are produced when they do appear.

SOCRATES. I have a suspicion, Meno, that you and I are not much good. Our masters Gorgias and Prodicus have not trained us properly. We must certainly take ourselves in hand, and try to find someone who will improve us by
E   hook or by crook. I say this with our recent discussion in mind, for absurdly enough we failed to perceive that it is not only under the guidance of knowledge that human action is well and rightly conducted. I believe that may be what prevents us from seeing how it is that men are made good.

MENO. What do you mean?

SOCRATES. This. We were correct, were we not, in agreeing that good men must be profitable or useful? It cannot
97 be otherwise, can it?

MENO. No.

SOCRATES. And again that they will be of some use if they conduct our affairs aright – that also was correct?

MENO. Yes.

SOCRATES. But in insisting that knowledge was a *sine qua non* for right leadership, we look like being mistaken.

MENO. How so?

SOCRATES. Let me explain. If someone knows the way to Larissa, or anywhere else you like, then when he goes there and takes others with him he will be a good and capable guide, you would agree?

MENO. Of course.

SOCRATES. But if a man judges correctly which is the road, though he has never been there and doesn't know it, will he not also guide others aright? **B**

MENO. Yes, he will.

SOCRATES. And as long as he has a correct opinion on the points about which the other has knowledge, he will be just as good a guide, believing the truth but not knowing it.

MENO. Just as good.

SOCRATES. Therefore true opinion is as good a guide as knowledge for the purpose of acting rightly. That is what we left out just now in our discussion of the nature of virtue, when we said that knowledge is the only guide to right action. There was also, it seems, true opinion. **C**

MENO. It seems so.

SOCRATES. So right opinion is something no less useful than knowledge.

MENO. Except that the man with knowledge will always be successful, and the man with right opinion only sometimes.

SOCRATES. What? Will he not always be successful so long as he has the right opinion?

MENO. That must be so, I suppose. In that case, I wonder why knowledge should be so much more prized than right opinion, and indeed how there is any difference between them. **D**

SOCRATES. Shall I tell you the reason for your surprise, or do you know it?

MENO. No, tell me.

SOCRATES. It is because you have not observed the statues of Daedalus. Perhaps you don't have them in your country.

MENO. What makes you say that?

SOCRATES. They too, if no one ties them down, run away and escape. If tied, they stay where they are put.

B MENO. What of it?

SOCRATES. If you have one of his works untethered, it is not worth much: it gives you the slip like a runaway slave. But a tethered specimen is very valuable, for they are magnificent creations. And that, I may say, has a bearing on the matter of true opinions. True opinions are a fine thing and do all sorts of good so long as they

98 stay in their place; but they will not stay long. They run away from a man's mind, so they are not worth much until you tether them by working out the reason. That process, my dear Meno, is recollection, as we agreed earlier. Once they are tied down, they become knowledge, and are stable. That is why knowledge is something more valuable than right opinion. What distinguishes one from the other is the tether.

MENO. It does seem something like that, certainly.

B SOCRATES. Well of course, I have only been using an analogy myself, not knowledge. But it is not, I am sure, a mere guess to say that right opinion and knowledge are different. There are few things that I should claim to know, but that at least is among them, whatever else is.

MENO. You are quite right.

SOCRATES. And is this right too, that true opinion when it governs any course of action produces as good a result as knowledge?

MENO. Yes, that too is right, I think.

C SOCRATES. So that for practical purposes right opinion is no less useful than knowledge, and the man who has it is no less useful than the one who knows.

MENO. That is so.

SOCRATES. Now we have agreed that the good man is useful.

MENO. Yes.

SOCRATES. To recapitulate then: assuming that there are

men good and useful to the community, it is not only knowledge that makes them so, but also right opinion, and neither of these comes by nature but both are acquired – or do you think either of them *is* natural?

MENO. No.

SOCRATES. So if both are acquired, good men themselves are not good by nature.

MENO. No.

SOCRATES. That being so, the next thing we inquired was whether their goodness was a matter of teaching, and we decided that it would be, if virtue were knowledge, and conversely, that if it could be taught, it would be knowledge.

MENO. Yes.

SOCRATES. Next, that if there were teachers of it, it could be taught, but not if there were none.

MENO. That was so.

SOCRATES. But we have agreed that there are no teachers of it, and so that it cannot be taught and is not knowledge.

MENO. We did.

SOCRATES. At the same time we agreed that it is something good, and that to be useful and good consists in giving right guidance.

MENO. Yes.

SOCRATES. And that these two, true opinion and knowledge, are the only things which direct us aright and the possession of which makes a man a true guide. We may except chance, because what turns out right by chance is not due to human direction, and say that where human control leads to right ends, these two principles are directive, true opinion and knowledge.

MENO. Yes, I agree.

SOCRATES. Now since virtue cannot be taught, we can no longer believe it to be knowledge, so that one of our two good and useful principles is excluded, and knowledge is not the guide in public life.

MENO. No.

SOCRATES. It is not then by the possession of any wisdom that such men as Themistocles, and the others whom Anytus mentioned just now, became leaders in their cities. This fact, that they do not owe their eminence to knowledge, will explain why they are unable to make others like themselves.

MENO. No doubt it is as you say.

SOCRATES. That leaves us with the other alternative, that it is well-aimed conjecture which statesmen employ in upholding their countries' welfare. Their position in relation to knowledge is no different from that of prophets and tellers of oracles, who under divine inspiration utter many truths, but have no knowledge of what they are saying.

MENO. It must be something like that.

SOCRATES. And ought we not to reckon those men divine who with no conscious thought are repeatedly and outstandingly successful in what they do or say?

MENO. Certainly.

SOCRATES. We are right therefore to give this title to the oracular priests and the prophets that I mentioned, and to poets of every description. Statesmen too, when by their speeches they get great things done yet know nothing of what they are saying, are to be considered as acting no less under divine influence, inspired and possessed by the divinity.

MENO. Certainly.

SOCRATES. Women, you know, Meno, do call good men 'divine', and the Spartans too, when they are singing a good man's praises, say 'He is divine'.

MENO. And it looks as if they are right – though our friend Anytus may be annoyed with you for saying so.

SOCRATES. I can't help that. We will talk to him some other time. If all we have said in this discussion, and the questions we have asked, have been right, virtue will be acquired neither by nature nor by teaching. Whoever has it gets it by divine dispensation without taking thought, unless he be the kind of statesman who can create another like himself. Should there be such a man, he would be among the living practically what Homer said Tiresias was among the dead, when he described him as the only one in the underworld who kept his wits – 'the others are mere flitting shades'. Where virtue is concerned such a man would be just like that, a solid reality among shadows.

MENO. That is finely put, Socrates.

SOCRATES. On our present reasoning then, whoever has virtue gets it by divine dispensation. But we shall not understand the truth of the matter until, before asking how men get virtue, we try to discover what virtue is in and by itself. Now it is time for me to go; and my request to you is that you will allay the anger of your friend Anytus by convincing him that what you now believe is true. If you succeed, the Athenians may have cause to thank you.

SUGGESTIONS FOR FURTHER READING

GENERAL INTRODUCTION TO GREEK PHILOSOPHY

A. H. Armstrong, *An Introduction to Ancient Philosophy*, Methuen, 4th ed. 1965

W. K. C. Guthrie, *The Greek Philosophers from Thales to Aristotle*, Methuen's University Paperbacks 1967 (originally published 1950).

F. M. Cornford, *Before and After Socrates*, Cambridge University Press 1932 (and later in paperback).

PLATO

G. C. Field, *The Philosophy of Plato*, Oxford University Press (Home University Library) 1949.

G. C. Field, *Plato and his Contemporaries*, Methuen 1930.

R. S. Bluck, *Plato's Life and Thought*, Routledge 1949.

G. M. A. Grube, *Plato's Thought*, Methuen 1935.

More advanced is I. M. Crombie, *An Examination of Plato's Doctrines*, 2 vols., Routledge 1962 and 1963.

Useful bibliographies will be found in Armstrong's book and Field's *Philosophy of Plato*.

Plato in Penguin Classics

A Selection

THE REPUBLIC
Translated by Desmond Lee

Here Plato attempts to apply the principles of his philosophy to political affairs. Ostensibly a discussion on the nature of Justice, *The Republic* lays before us Plato's vision of the ideal state, and includes some of his most important writing on the nature of reality and the theory of the 'forms'.

THE LAWS
Translated by T. J. Saunders

The rigours of life in Plato's utopian Republic are not much tempered here, but *The Laws*, depicting a society permeated by the rule of law, is a much more practical approach to Plato's ideal.

THE SYMPOSIUM
Translated by Walter Hamilton

This masterpiece of dramatic dialogue is set at a dinner party to which are invited several of the literary celebrities of Athenian society. After dinner, it is proposed that each member of the company should make a speech in praise of love.

GORGIAS
Translated by Walter Hamilton

Although Gorgias was a Sicilian teacher of oratory, the dialogue is more concerned with ethics than with the art of public speaking. Its chief interest lies less in Gorgias courteous outline of his art, than in the clash between Socrates, the true philosopher, and Callicles, a young Athenian of the stamp of Alcibiades, who brashly maintains that might is right.